Computer Systems Development

STrategic Resource Information Planning and Execution—STRIPE

DENIS A. CONNOR

PRENTICE HALL, Englewood Cliffs, NJ 07632

Library of Congress Cataloging-in-Publication Data

CONNOR, DENIS.
   Computer systems development.

   Includes index.
   1. Information resources management.   I. Title.
T58.64.C66   1988   658.4'038'0285   87-35919
ISBN 0-13-162819-4

Editorial/production supervision and
   interior design: Arthur Maisel
Cover design: 20/20 Services, Inc.
Manufacturing buyer: Lorraine Fumoso

© 1988 by Prentice-Hall, Inc.
A Division of Simon & Schuster
Englewood Cliffs, New Jersey 07632

Printed in the United States of America

10   9   8   7   6   5   4   3   2   1

ISBN 0-13-162819-4

Prentice-Hall International (UK) Limited, *London*
Prentice-Hall of Australia Pty. Limited, *Sydney*
Prentice-Hall Canada Inc., *Toronto*
Prentice-Hall Hispanoamericana, S.A., *Mexico*
Prentice-Hall of India Private Limited, *New Delhi*
Prentice-Hall of Japan, Inc., *Tokyo*
Prentice-Hall of Southeast Asia Pte. Ltd., *Singapore*
Editora Prentice-Hall do Brasil, Ltda., *Rio de Janeiro*

To Constance, my wife

Contents

Preface

This book was written to give individuals responsible for providing effective information systems support a framework for all work done in this area. This framework encompasses strategic, tactical, and operational planning and implementation, information resource management, data driven systems design, and design and development of the technical environment.

Many organizations today have concluded that their present computer systems do not effectively meet their present and future needs. Their systems maintenance costs run as high as 80 percent of their total management information services' staffing budgets, and any new application development is directed at particular user needs and is not part of an overall long-range or strategic plan. Further, their data are application oriented and have no foundation in a corporate logical data structure. This situation, compounded with more computer conscious and computer knowledgeable users, is a major concern to senior management.

These problems cannot be solved overnight. STRIPE (Strategic Resource Information Planning and Execution) has been developed as a long-term solution. STRIPE is a matrix-driven methodology which is intended to provide management information services (MIS) with a tool to plan and control computer systems development and its allied functions. This is done through the strategic, tactical, and operational planning and implementation in terms of the business, its data and applications, and its technical (systems) environment.

The essential difference between the STRIPE matrix approach and other similar methodologies is that it is the only one which integrates all three planning levels. For example, many different methodologies are available for strategic information planning, information resource management and application system development. The enterprise then has to piece them together.

STRIPE may be viewed from three directions. The first is the STRIPE matrix (Table 1.1 in the text). This matrix may be termed the "output" view as it lists all the outputs provided by MIS at each of the three planning levels and indicates which STRIPE phases produce them. The second is the STRIPE methodology Table of Contents (Appendix B). This is the "micro" view and because it provides a sequence of events, it is ideal for developing project plans and schedules. The third is the "macro" view and is the description of each STRIPE activity and, where needed, the theory behind the activity. This is the hands-on support found in the body of the text.

Because STRIPE is based on a matrix of outputs, it can be used in total or only in terms of specific outputs and their related activities. For example, it can be used to develop a strategic information plan, establish an information resource management framework, define a technical architecture or develop data-driven application systems. Further, if an organization is very large, STRIPE can be applied at the division or even at the level of a major business application.

Techniques of particular interest described in the text are the development of the strategic information plan, top-down data modeling derived from the information architecture and bottom-up through canonical synthesis, a data-driven system design technique based on data analysis and real-world actions, and prototyping using an expanding data model. (Data are added to the data model as the business functions are expanded.) These techniques are easily learned and can be applied immediately in the organization.

The STRIPE techniques combined with a fourth generation language/data base management system and a data dictionary provide extremely powerful and effective planning, system design and development tools. They get to the root of the problem and eliminate hours of labor used in conventional process-driven approaches.

These techniques provide a new twist to the subject of system design as described by authors such as James Martin, Tom deMarco, Ed Yourdon, Ken Orr, and Michael Jackson. I discussed and compared their design techniques against a single case study in *Information System Specification and Design Road Map,* Prentice-Hall, Inc., 1985.

The STRIPE methodology could be applied as written or used with the system development methodology in any organization. This is achieved by first matching the outputs from the organization's methodology with the outputs in the STRIPE matrix. The methodology activities for those outputs that match are then compared with the corresponding STRIPE activities and are modified as appropriate. Finally, the STRIPE outputs which are not found in the organization's methodology are reviewed to determine whether the methodology should be expanded to include them. Since most application system development methodologies (ASDMs) apply to the system life-cycle activities, in Chapters 7, 8, 9, 11 and 12 the appropriate STRIPE phases are matched to generic ASDM phases.

The STRIPE audience includes those organizations that wish to move into a user responsive data-driven systems environment. This textbook should be read by managers, strategic planning analysts, users, systems analysts, data administrators, and data processing auditors. STRIPE would be especially valuable to those introducing the use of fourth generation techniques into an organization.

Denis Connor

Acknowledgments

This book took over two years to develop and in the process went through several versions, which I used as class manuals to teach and apply the STRIPE methodology and its related techniques. My students were probably my best critics and helped me refine much of the material described here, when it was applied to their own organizations' problems during the workshop sessions. I thank all of them for their help and regret that there are too many to name individually.

Three individuals I owe a debt of gratitude to are my editor, Pat Henry, Dave D'Braunstein from California Federal, and Ken Peddle from Price Waterhouse. All three took great pains to read the material in detail and offer both constructive criticism and suggestions to improve the presentation of the subject matter. Ken Peddle, in particular, edited my final manuscript and polished the wording so that it is now much clearer and easier to read and understand.

1
Introduction

It is rapidly becoming accepted that strategic planning of an organization's future direction is a must for survival. In the private sector, corporate management is becoming aware that an organization can no longer survive against its competition without clearly defined strategic plans for at least three to five years into the future. In the public sector, competition is replaced by deficit budgets, and critical communications media representing the general population which demand improved levels of productivity for their tax dollars.

Even though the realization of the need for strategic planning exists, most organizations do not know how to approach the problem. The larger companies and governments tend to go to consultants to provide this expertise. The smaller companies find it difficult to justify this type of expense, particularly as the return on investment cannot be easily quantified. Further, whether the organization is large or small, the return on investment occurs often months or years down the road. So, today's problems attract the most attention. As a result, though many agree that strategic planning is essential, few actually do it.

In any event, what does corporate strategic planning mean to the information systems department? In fact, don't we have enough problems trying to maintain existing application systems and to satisfy the ever increasing demands of the users for new applications? Users, who now believe they know all about system design because they have a product like Lotus 1-2-3 on their PCs. Or, the company may be losing money and would it not be wiser at this time to freeze all new development and just make sure the present applications continue to operate? Possibly, there may even be some quick and dirty solutions? Maybe these new fourth generation languages combined with powerful data base management systems could solve all systems problems? Don't the vendors claim their products can almost work miracles?

On the other hand, senior management has become acutely aware of the high hardware, software and personnel overhead associated with computerized information processing. This high cost has brought the information systems department to the forefront of corporate management's consciousness. They also realize that data processing is the heart of the organization and the enterprise cannot survive without management information systems. Sounds familiar, doesn't it? Well, what can we do about it?

The first step is to acknowledge problems exist in information processing. Without this acknowledgment, strategic planning becomes a meaningless exercise where only the motions are executed and no worthwhile results achieved. The second step is to develop solutions using a management information services (MIS) strategic plan to determine where you should be headed in three to five years and to get you there safely. The third step is to develop tactical plans defining the specific projects and functions to be carried out during a specific time frame, such as a fiscal year. The fourth step is to plan each project in detail and execute it.

Before we develop the solutions, let's define the problems in greater detail.

1.1 THE PROBLEMS

In most organizations, many business applications have been put on the computer and appear to function adequately. For example, checks go out on time, information is available on computer terminals and all kinds of reports are produced and distributed. In this context, why should senior management not be satisfied with the status quo? Why should they consider the development and implementation of strategic plans for their MIS function? On the surface, everything may appear to be smooth sailing. But what is the real situation?

Operating Costs

In many companies, the cost of MIS including hardware, software and people amounts to 10 to 20 percent of the operating budget. It makes business sense to increase productivity in this area. Further, a major portion of the

MIS cost, from a third to a half, is the cost of system development staff, such as systems analysts and programmers, data base analysts and other support staff. And of this system development cost, 75 to 90 percent is spent on maintaining current systems, either for correcting errors in programs or for modifying these systems to meet changing user requirements. Major new system development costs can sometimes be equal to or exceed the maintenance costs. Some organizations fund this development through special one-time allocations, which can become self-perpetuating.

New Development

New system development takes an unacceptable amount of elapsed time, often years, and actual costs exceed originally approved budgets by wide margins. Further, when put into production, these systems require major modifications to meet the user's needs which have either changed or not been properly understood when the system was designed. This problem occurs because user management does not understand the system development process, and MIS management compounds the situation by making firm commitments when available information is imprecise.

Management Information

Management decision support data are not readily available and must be compiled manually or by feeding operating information into microcomputers and manipulating it there.

Why do these problems exist and how can they be solved? They exist for a variety of reasons which include data, programming languages, dependencies and system life-cycle control.

Data.   Most organizations do not have a corporate view of data. Instead, every business application has its own files in which data inconsistency, redundancy and incompatibility are rampant.

What do these terms mean? Data inconsistency occurs when multiple applications use the same data but with different names and shades of meaning. Data redundancy occurs when the same data are stored in different files. As a result, file updates do not occur simultaneously and information extracted from different files for different purposes contain different data. Data incompatibility occurs when data are structured differently in different files requiring complex interfaces to pass data to and fro.

This problem is made worse when data base management systems have been used to store individual application files. Data dictionaries which can store information about records, data elements, programs, and modules, are rarely used. The widespread use of microcomputers has also contributed to a climate for data inconsistency, redundancy and incompatibility.

Programming languages.   Most current programs are coded in a procedural language such as COBOL or PL1. (A procedural language uses "how" type instructions; a nonprocedural language uses "what" type instructions). Procedural languages are more complex to use than nonprocedural languages and can result in:

- large numbers of programmers being needed,
- the need for systems analysts to interface between the users and the programmers,
- higher education costs,
- difficulties in program testing, and
- the need for manually creating supporting program documentation.

On the other hand, nonprocedural languages (commonly referred to as fourth generation languages) are often machine inefficient and cannot cope with complex procedural logic.

Though it is inappropriate to discuss detailed solutions at this point, it is worth noting that many organizations have achieved considerable programming success using high level procedural languages such as IBM's Cross System Product (CSP), Cincom's MANTIS, ADR's IDEAL and Software AG's NATURAL. Another product is Paul Bassett's FRAME technology, which is marketed by Netron under the CAP (Computer Automated Programming) umbrella. This tool, using artificial intelligence, makes programming with any procedural language very simple and efficient. At present the language being supported is COBOL in the IBM and Wang environments. In the future, Bassett FRAMES can be expected to displace many so-called fourth generation languages because the FRAMES are simple to use and have all the power and efficiency of procedural languages.

Dependencies.   Strong dependencies exist between data and program code because the data are buried in the code. Hence, changes to data require major program changes. Strong dependencies also exist between program modules. Hence, changes in any one module create a ripple effect throughout the system.

System life-cycle control.   Management of the system life cycle from the identification of the need for the system to phasing out or replacement of the system is either casually managed or overcontrolled. In the first situation, the designers and developers are given a free rein to do as they please. In the second, controls are rigidly imposed through the mandatory use of application system development methodologies which are either developed in-house or acquired from external suppliers. The latter become a problem when they restrict the use of more effective system design techniques because they do not fit the standards imposed by the methodology.

1.2 SOLUTIONS THROUGH STRATEGIC, TACTICAL AND OPERATIONAL PLANNING

These problems can be solved by developing and implementing effective strategic, tactical and operational plans for the management information services department within the organization. These three planning levels should be developed in a highly structured and organized manner. They should incorporate techniques for analyzing business functions, developing across-the-corporation views of data and using this information to design and build application systems to meet both present and future business needs.

The Strategic Information Resource Plan (SIRP)

This plan is developed by MIS management to define where MIS should be in three to five years, and to organize and control migration from the present environment to this defined goal. This strategic plan covers five phases: (1) definition of the company's business in terms of its business strategy, (2) the development of its information architecture, (3) the design of the supporting technical architecture, (4) the development of a migration strategy, and (5) the conversion of the initial projects into a set of tactical plans. On completion of the initial SIRP, this strategic plan must be periodically reviewed and kept up to date at least every half year.

Tactical Plans

The tactical plans provide the bridge between specific projects, such as developing specific application systems, or acquiring and installing hardware and software, and the strategic plan. They are similar to the plans usually prepared with specific budgets for a fiscal year.

Operational Plans

The operational plans are the specific detailed plans for each project.

1.3 STRATEGIC RESOURCE INFORMATION PLANNING AND
EXECUTION (STRIPE)

The task of developing strategic, tactical and operational plans becomes much easier when a road map is available which defines specific activities to be executed. The planning and implementation become more effective when supported by simple data modeling, and application system design and development techniques. These techniques must reflect the corporate view of the organization's data and permit user participation in system prototyping. STRIPE (Strategic Resource Information Planning and Execution) is a complete methodology which has been developed as a set of techniques and procedures to encompass all three levels of planning, with emphasis on information resource management and application systems development.

Table 1.1 is a matrix which displays the STRIPE outputs. These are grouped under business, data, applications, technical environment, and type of plan in terms of strategic, tactical and operational planning.

This book describes the techniques and procedures which make STRIPE unique. These include all aspects of strategic planning, information resource management, and application system design and development. The tactical and operational activities associated with the technical environment are straightforward and hence, are not discussed.

The appendices contain the detailed case study referenced in the text. They also contain the STRIPE methodology's Table of Contents.

STRIPE is easily followed and can be applied immediately in an organization. It provides a logical sequence of activities commencing with the development of the strategic information resource plan (SIRP), the detailed design of the information architecture and implementation of information resource management, the design of the technical architecture and the development of the technical environment, and the design and development of new interactive systems directly from the data defined in the data models by using system prototyping.

The matrix approach used in the methodology makes it highly flexible. All or part of it can be used to meet users' particular needs. For example, an organization interested in information resource management only would need the business strategy (SP1), the major functions (SP2), the data architecture (SP2), function expansion (TP1) and logical data base design (TP2). Another interested in application system development would need the application architecture (SP2), the current application evaluation (SP4), physical application definition (TP3) and all the operational outputs except OP11. Needless to say, the matrix drives home the fact that the outputs defined in it make up a whole and any specific set within it must be viewed as part of that whole.

STRIPE techniques eliminate hours of labor required by conventional system planning and design methods such as the drawing of data flows and

TABLE 1.1 The Stripe Matrix

	Business	Data	Application	Technical Environment	Type of Plan
STRATEGIC PLANNING	SP1 Business Strategy: Mission, Objectives and Goals, Strategic Directions, Critical Success Factors (CSFs), Major Information Requirements; SP2 Major Functions (Processes); SP4 User and MIS Department Evaluation; SP4 Proposed Organizations	SP2 Data Architecture: Primary Entities, Crown, E-R Diagram, Subject Data Bases	SP2 Application Architecture: Business Applications; SP4 Current Application Evaluation	SP3 Technical Architecture: Function Distribution, Computers and Peripherals, Data Distribution, Communications, Software (DBMS, Dictionary, Security), Office Automation; SP4 Evaluation of Current Hardware/Software, Communications and Office Automation	SP4 Migration Plan: Major Projects over a 3–5 year period
TACTICAL PLANNING	TP1 Function Expansion; TP1 ASDM Policy; TP1 Organization Change: IRM Function, Education Function, Strategic Planning Function, Quality Assurance	TP2 Logical Data Bases: Entity Expansion, Current Files/Documents Comparison, Data Normalization, Data Distribution	TP3 Physical Application Definition	TP4 Hardware/Software Communications/Office Automation Specifications; TP5 Selection of: Computers, etc., Communications Equipment, Software, Office Automation Equipment and Software	SP5 Budget Year Plan: (or similar period) Prioritized Projects scheduled and resourced
OPERATIONAL PLANNING	OP2 Business System Specifications: Activity Level Functions, Output Requirements, Output Design; OP9 System Implementation: Manual Procedures, D.P. Operations Procedures, Education; OP7 System Test: Testing; OP10 System Review: Business Needs, Operating Efficiency	OP4 Physical Data Base Design: Activity Level, Data Expansion, Data Volumes, Data Accesses, Physical Data Bases, Physical DB Access Modules; OP7 Testing; OP9 File Conversion	OP3 Procedure Design: Event and External Action/Condition Analysis, Embryonic Procedures, Menu Hierarchies, Input Screens and Forms; OP5 Procedure Expansion: File Update Logic, Output Logic; OP6 System Construction: Physical Procedures; OP8 Package Acquisition; OP7 System Test: Testing; OP9 Production Libraries	OP11 Product Implementation: Product Acquisition, Product Installation, Product Conversion, Product Testing	OP1 Individual Project Plans

Warnier/Orr diagrams, and structure charts. Combined with effective fourth generation procedural and nonprocedural languages, data base management systems and a data dictionary/encyclopedia, they provide extremely powerful and effective planning, system design and development tools.

STRIPE techniques are described in the context of the complete methodology and associated with the particular activity to be executed. Thus, the reader is given a set of tools and is shown when, where and how to use them. The single exception to this rule is the description of the strategic information resource plan. The related activities are found in Appendix B—The STRIPE methodology Table of Contents.

The strategic information resource plan (SIRP) is discussed in terms of its content and how the outputs may be obtained rather than as a set of activities. This is done as it is important that the SIRP be viewed as a set of strategies rather than as a set of activities. Once the concepts have been understood, the STRIPE activities can be easily planned and executed.

1.4 BENEFITS OF USING STRIPE

Why use STRIPE? It provides:

- a matrix approach to strategic, tactical and operational planning in terms of the business, data, applications, the technical environment and the type of plan. This matrix points to the procedures used to provide required outputs. The independence of each procedure is preserved;
- the basis for establishing a strategic information resource plan for the MIS organization;
- simple techniques to build corporate data models and subject data bases which mirror an organization's business;
- a mechanism to map data bases to application systems which simplifies and reduces the work and time involved in system development and maintenance;
- a natural, evolutionary process for doing system prototyping to increase the understanding of an organization's functions and data;
- a planned technical environment to support the entire organization and its information architecture.

REFERENCES

1. Cross System Product (CSP) software marketed by IBM, order numbers SBOF–1023 and SBOF–1024.

2. MANTIS software marketed by Cincom, 2300 Montana Avenue, Cincinnati, OH 45211.

3. IDEAL software marketed by Applied Data Research, Inc., Route 206 and Orchard Road, CN-5, Princeton, NJ 08540.

4. NATURAL software marketed by Software AG of North America, Inc., Reston International Center, 11800 Sunrise Valley Drive, Reston, VA 22091.

5. NETRON/CAP software marketed by Netron Inc., 99 St. Regis Cresent North, Downsview, Ontario M3J 1Y9, Canada.

2
Management of the STRIPE Process

STRIPE includes the development, implementation and maintenance of the MIS strategic plan (SIRP), and the tactical and operational plans. These plans describe the development and maintenance of the information architecture, the technical architecture and application systems. The planning activities are usually done by a temporary group initially and by permanent groups over the longer term.

After completing the original strategic information resource planning (SIRP) project, MIS functions which may be introduced include planning, information resource management, the information center and quality assurance. The current functions which may change are discrete planning of application systems, hardware, software and communication networks, the data administration function, and application systems development and maintenance. Let's discuss the new functions.

2.1 PLANNING

The concept of strategic planning for MIS is different from the annual planning of application systems based on user requests for enhancements to existing systems and new systems, and the resulting need to increase processing and storage capacities, set up additional communication networks and acquire more sophisticated software. Annual planning is generally done only for the budget year. Strategic planning extends over several years and is based on the organization's business strategy for the same period. It also includes the monitoring and replanning of projects defined in the strategic plan.

The SIRP scope defines the limits of the strategic planning project. This could include the entire organization, the corporate level only, a division level or a function level. In very large organizations, it may be worthwhile developing the SIRP at two levels at least, the first plan at the corporate level and the second at a division or function level. The corporate level SIRP would provide an umbrella for the lower level strategic plans.

Both the initial strategic planning project, the ongoing planning function and the review of all projects should be directed and controlled by a subcommittee of company vice-presidents called a steering or review committee. This committee should ensure that the MIS strategic plan is in line with the company's business strategy. Direct control of planning and implementation should be by one of the vice-presidents on the steering committee. Should the SIRP not be at the corporate level, then the steering committee should be drawn from the senior-most levels of management within the area to be studied.

The original SIRP project team should be relatively small and not exceed six members who should be drawn from the user, the data administration and the system development staff. The small team size will provide a close working relationship between the members and reduce the administrative overhead that comes with large teams. Additional expertise and support in specific areas during the SIRP project may be obtained from permanent staff.

The success of the SIRP project is dependent on the project team's knowledge and understanding of the planning requirements and the processes to be used. Prior experience in strategic information planning would be an asset. Before the SIRP project is started, all the team members should be familiar with all aspects of STRIPE. In particular, the detailed process to be followed during strategic planning should be well understood.

The SIRP project should be planned as a major project with costs, schedules, activities and tasks identified. Planning and review sessions with the review committee should be scheduled at the beginning and end of each phase.

Table 2.1 is a sample project work plan for the SIRP. The table column headings are the STRIPE activity number; the day number commencing from the first working day of the project; the resources planned to be used in person days for each team member such as a senior consultant, a consultant, users 1 & 2, a senior systems analyst, and any other staff involved; and a comments column with such information as the group responsible for the

TABLE 2.1 PROJECT WORK PLAN
CALENDAR SCHEDULE AND COMPONENT WORK LOAD

Activity	Day No. From	Day No. To	Senior Consultant	Consultant	User #1	User #2	Senior Systems Analyst	Other Staff	Comments
			Resources in Person Days						
Start-up Phase									
SUP. 1	1	1	0.5	0.5	0.5	0.5	0.5	4.5	Review Board
SUP. 2	1	1	0.5	0.5	0.5	0.5	0.5	2	Systems Coordinator
SUP. 3	2	2	1	1	1	1	1	9	Review Board
SUP. 4	3	7	5	5	5	5	5	?	Project Team Selected DP Staff Users
Subtotal			7	7	7	7	7	?	
PHASE 1 The Business Strategy									
SP1. A	8	8	1	1	1	1	1	4	Systems Coordinator
SP1. B	9	9	1	1	1	1	1	?	Senior Staff as Required
SP1. .1	10	14	5	5	5	5	5	4	Systems Coordinator
SP1. X	15	17	2	2	3	3	3	9	Review Board
SP1. Y	22	22	1	1	1	1	1		
SP1. Z	24	25	1	1	1	1	1	?	
Subtotal			11	10	12	11	11	?	

PHASE 2   The Information Architecture

SP2 A	18	18	1	1	1	1	4	Systems Coordinator
SP2 B	19	19	1	1	1	1	?	Systems Development
SP2 .1	20	28	5	5	5	5	5	Office Systems Support
- SP2 .6								Data Administrator
SP2 .7	29	29	1	1	1	1	?	Data Administrator
SP2 .8	30	32	2	3	3	3	?	Data Administrator
-SP2 .11								Data Administrator
SP2 .12	33	35	3	3	3	3	?	Data Administrator
- SP2 .13								
SP2 .14	36	37	1	3	3	3	?	Data Administrator
SP2 .15	38	38	1	1	1	1	?	Systems Management
SP2 X	39	43	3	5	5	5	4	Systems Coordinator
SP2 Y	48	48	1	1	1	1	9	Review Board
SP2 Z	50	51	1	1	1	1		
Subtotal	20	14	25	24	24		?	

activity. This information is provided for the activities involved in each phase and the phase is subtotaled. At the end of the plan, the total time for each individual is recorded.

The entire ideal elapsed time for the SIRP project should be about six months. The six-month time frame is suggested because the plan is at the strategic level only. Elapsed time for tactical and operational projects that follow the strategic plan will depend on the degree of complexity involved and the size of each project.

On completion of the project, a permanent planning group should be established to be responsible for monitoring the implementation of the strategic plan and updating it at periodic intervals (six months to one year) to ensure it is always in line with the company's business strategies. This group would also assist MIS line managers in developing their tactical plans, and in planning each operational project in detail.

Each of the tactical and operational projects should have an individual responsible for coordination with the planning group to ensure that these plans and schedules stay within the framework of the SIRP.

The SIRP project manager should be the individual who will become the permanent manager of MIS planning. It is possible that no suitable person may be available in the company to serve as project manager and the organization may feel that a consultant with the proper experience and knowledge may be more appropriate. If this should happen, then the consultant must be made responsible for training his or her replacement on the project to continue as the permanent manager.

2.2 INFORMATION RESOURCE MANAGEMENT (IRM)

The management of information as a resource is as critical in an organization as the management of its finances, its products or its people. Information resource management (IRM) is an approach to identify, organize and structure an organization's decision making, control and operational data based on an analysis of:

- the organization's mission and purpose,
- management's strategic, tactical and operational business objectives,
- critical success factors (CSFs),
- strategic directions,
- high-level information requirements, and
- existing data as recorded in computer and manual files.

The expected results from IRM are sets or clusters of data grouped logically and physically together to enable application systems to be built to keep the data current, and to provide access to them in human readable form such as screens, reports, checks, invoices, and so forth.

These sets of data can be referred to as data bases. A data base is a file which has a defined logical or physical structure in which data are stored according to this structure. The logical structure is the view the user has of the structure. It can be part or all of the data in a single physical data base or can cross physical data base boundaries. The physical structure is the way the data are organized and stored in a physical medium such as a disk file.

Application system development (ASD) is the development and maintenance of an application system throughout its life cycle, that is, from the time the need for the system was identified to its obsolescence. (Maintenance includes the changing or enhancing of the system to meet current and future needs.) Application systems are built to provide information that enables the organization to carry out its business functions effectively. Application systems record, update, and extract data defined in the organization's data architecture.

Most MIS departments today have distinct system development and maintenance sections. Some also have data administration sections and a few have planning staff. This type of organization is based on the premise that the planners plan; the system developers design, build and maintain application systems; and the data administration staff control the data in the data dictionary. The problem is not that the necessary functions do not exist, as they usually do. The problem is that each function operates independently of the others. The joint efforts are not effectively directed at supplying the total information needs of the organization. In addition, each application has its own data files, and the concept of an information architecture reflecting the company's business as a whole usually does not exist.

The information resource management approach is based on the development of a corporate information architecture which includes both data and application architectures. This information architecture becomes the foundation for the development of application systems and physical data bases. The MIS department's organizational structure should reflect this approach and include an IRM to manage the company's data and design its logical application systems. The actual physical system development should remain the responsibility of the system development section.

2.3 THE INFORMATION CENTER

Data updating, such as addition, deletion or change in value, can be separated from data extraction. MIS should be responsible for all data update functions within applications, and possibly certain critical data extraction functions such as check writing. All ad hoc data extraction functions could be developed and maintained by the users. The delegation of this responsibility to the user community becomes achievable through the use of data base management systems and fourth generation languages.

This results in MIS becoming the true custodian of data in the organization. The users are free to produce decision support output they need to perform their functional responsibilities. The users should be supported in this activity by an information center group who are expert in the use of data extraction and manipulation (report writing) software. This group should provide education to the users in the use of the software and resolve problems they encounter.

2.4 QUALITY ASSURANCE

Quality assurance implies that the product meets certain standards or criteria. These standards are often viewed quantitatively, such as forms completed, rather than qualitatively, such as users' needs effectively met. This occurs because it is far easier to do the former. Effective quality assurance encompasses both the development of qualitative and quantitative standards in MIS and the measurement of the product in terms of these standards.

In terms of STRIPE, these standards should define the specifications of the STRIPE matrix outputs and elaborate on the activities used to produce them. Standards should also be developed to measure the use of resources such as people time and machine resources to ensure that projects are not planned and executed in unreasonable time frames and using unlimited computer power. In terms of user satisfaction, the STRIPE concepts increase the probability that the final product will meet the users' needs satisfactorily.

3
The STRIPE Methodology

The strategic resource information planning and execution (STRIPE) methodology was developed to provide management information services (MIS) with a tool to plan and control computer systems development and its allied functions through strategic, tactical and operational planning. This methodology is driven by the outputs found in Table 1.1, the STRIPE matrix.

To supplement this textbook, a set of detailed procedures has been developed. These procedures are organized by phases and activities which provide the critical outputs in each entity category. Appendix B lists the complete Table of Contents for the methodology procedures. Further, a subset of this Table of Contents and a highlighted matrix precedes each chapter of this book which discusses these procedures.

Each procedure is complete and independent and includes the individual(s) responsible for the procedure, those approving and those participating, the inputs and where they come from, the process to be followed, and the outputs. Comments are also included to put the procedure in context and to make it clearer. Figures 3.1 and 3.2 are illustrations of these procedures.

In the STRIPE matrix, though the outputs are grouped by category, they are produced at different times and sequences. For example, the definition of the business strategy occurs during the business strategy definition phase (SP1) while the user and MIS evaluation occurs during the migration

Activity SP2.1 - Identify the Organization's Functions

Staff Responsible	Project Manager Project Team
Staff Approval	Executive Sponsor
Staff Participation	Executive Management User Representatives User Middle Management Information Resource Management
Inputs	Organization Charts Procedure Manuals Job Descriptions Business Strategy Phase Report from SP1.Z
Process	Identify the highest level Functions in the company and expand these Functions to at least the middle management level of responsibility.
Outputs	Business Functions in the company
Comments	These Function Hierarchies may not reflect the people organization.

Figure 3.1   PHASE SP2   The Information Architecture

strategy phase (SP4), even though they are found together under "Business" at the strategic planning level.

In the matrix approach used in the STRIPE methodology, the developers are not faced with system flow diagrams at various levels, such as data flows, where they have to trace the flow of information through the different

Activity OP2.1 - Define Activity Level Functions

Staff Responsible	Information Resource Management Systems Designers
Staff Approval	Project Manager
Staff Participation	User Representatives User Middle Management
Inputs	Function Hierarchies from TP1.1
Process	Expand those Functions associated with the Application System being developed to the lowest Activity level needed to complete the expansion of the Data to meet all the business needs.
Outputs	Activity Level Functions
Comments	Programming control functions are not part of this Function expansion. Control Functions need only be identified during Activity OP6.1 - Design Physical Procedures.

Figure 3.2   PHASE OP2   Business System Specification

diagrams to understand the process. They can go directly to any planning level and to any output that relates to the business view, the data view, the application view, the technical environment view or the type of plan. From the chosen output, it is a simple matter to identify the relevant phase and activity that produce it. The activity then points to the input sources.

Further, the developers can choose to use all or just part of the matrix in terms of their particular needs. For example, if the major problem to be solved is to develop an information architecture, then only the business, data and application architecture categories are used. Or, if an information architecture is already available and the problem is interactive online system design, then Phases OP3 and OP5 in the application category are used.

Information on the methodology procedures may be obtained from Denis Connor and Associates, Inc., 83 Cathcart Crescent, Bramalea, Ontario, L6T 2A4.

4
The Strategic
Information Resource
Plan (SIRP)

A strategic information resource plan (SIRP) is developed by management information services (MIS) management to define where information services should be in three to five years, and to organize and control migration from the present environment to this defined goal. On completion of the initial SIRP, this strategic plan must be periodically reviewed and kept up to date at least every half year.

Table 4.1 highlights the outputs produced during the development of the SIRP. Some organizations may not be prepared to invest in the development of a SIRP for financial or other reasons, particularly as it is difficult to cost the benefits that could be accrued in hard dollars. In these circumstances, emphasis may be placed only on the information resource management aspects of the SIRP. These are covered in depth in Chapters 5 and 6.

TABLE 4.1 The STRIPE Matrix with Strategic Planning Phases Highlighted

	Business	Data	Application	Technical Environment	Type of Plan
STRATEGIC PLANNING	SP1 Business Strategy: Mission Objectives and Goals Strategic Directions Critical Success Factors (CSFs) Major Information Requirements SP2 Major Functions (Processes) SP4 User and MIS Department Evaluation SP4 Proposed Organizations	SP2 Data Architecture: Primary Entities Crown E-R Diagram Subject Data Bases	SP2 Application Architecture: Business Applications SP4 Current Application Evaluation	SP3 Technical Architecture: Function Distribution Computers and Peripherals Data Distribution Communications Software (DBMS, Dictionary. Security) Office Automation SP4 Evaluation of Current Hardware/Software, Communications and Office Automation	SP4 Migration Plan: Major Projects over a 3–5 year period
TACTICAL PLANNING	TP1 Function Expansion TP1 ASDM Policy TP1 Organization Change: IRM Function Education Function Strategic Planning Function Quality Assurance	TP2 Logical Data Bases: Entity Expansion Current Files/Documents Comparison Data Normalization Data Distribution	TP3 Physical Application Definition	TP4 Hardware/Software Communications/Office Automation Specifications TP5 Selection of: Computers, etc. Communications Equipment Software Office Automation Equipment and Software	SP5 Budget Year Plan: (or similar period) Prioritized Projects scheduled and resourced
OPERATIONAL PLANNING	OP2 Business System Specifications: Activity Level Functions Output Requirements Output Design OP9 System Implementation: Manual Procedures D.P. Operations Procedures Education OP7 System Test: Testing OP10 System Review: Business Needs Operating Efficiency	OP4 Physical Data Base Design: Activity Level Data Expansion Data Volumes Data Accesses Physical Data Bases Physical DB Access Modules OP7 Testing OP9 File Conversion	OP3 Procedure Design: Event and External Action/Condition Analysis Embryonic Procedures Menu Hierarchies Input Screens and Forms Procedure Expansion: File Update Logic Output Logic OP5 OP6 System Construction: Physical Procedures Package Acquisition OP8 OP7 System Test: Testing OP9 Production Libraries	OP11 Product Implementation: Product Acquisition Product Installation Product Conversion Product Testing	OP1 Individual Project Plans

21

The cost to an organization of not developing and maintaining an MIS strategic plan is that application systems will continue to be developed and maintained on a piecemeal basis and not as a reflection of the organization's business strategy.

4.1 THE SIRP PURPOSE AND OBJECTIVES

The MIS strategic plan must have a clearly defined purpose and a set of objectives. These are:

PURPOSE

- To relate the MIS functions to the corporate business strategies and to plan, develop and administer a strategic information resource plan (SIRP) over an extended period, for example, three to five years.

OBJECTIVES

- To record the organization's business strategies (if not already defined). This includes the organization's mission, objectives, critical success factors, assumptions about future directions and strategic plans.
- To develop an information architecture. This includes identification of functions and entities, conversion of the functions to applications, and the entities to entity-relationship diagrams and subject data bases, and to define the relationships between the applications and the subject data bases.
- To develop a technical architecture to provide the hardware, software and communications environment to implement the information architecture. This includes the computing requirements and the distribution of hardware, software and data.
- To develop a migration strategy to move from the present applications and technical environment to the future. This includes establishing the appropriate organization for implementation.
- To develop a set of tactical plans for implementation of the migration strategy over the short term (six months to one year). This includes hardware, software and communications selection, acquisition and installation, application development projects, file/data base conversions, and organization changes and education.

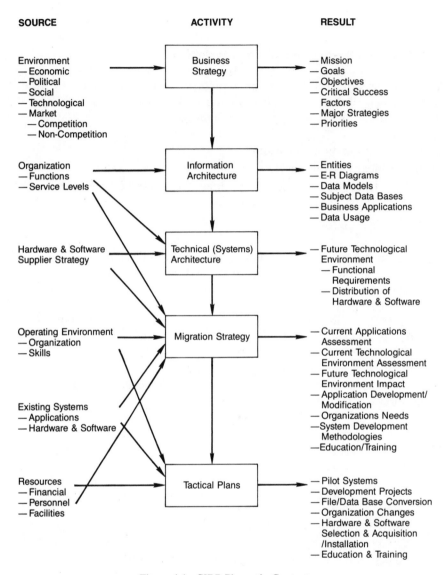

SOURCE   **ACTIVITY**   **RESULT**

Environment — Business Strategy — — Mission
— Economic — — Goals
— Political — — Objectives
— Social — — Critical Success
— Technological — Factors
— Market — — Major Strategies
— Competition — — Priorities
— Non-Competition

Organization — Information Architecture — — Entities
— Functions — — E-R Diagrams
— Service Levels — — Data Models
— Subject Data Bases
— Business Applications
— Data Usage

Hardware & Software Supplier Strategy — Technical (Systems) Architecture — — Future Technological Environment
— Functional Requirements
— Distribution of Hardware & Software

Operating Environment — Migration Strategy — — Current Applications Assessment
— Organization — — Current Technological Environment Assessment
— Skills — — Future Technological Environment Impact
— Application Development/ Modification
Existing Systems — — Organizations Needs
— Applications — —System Development Methodologies
— Hardware & Software — —Education/Training

Resources — Tactical Plans — — Pilot Systems
— Financial — — Development Projects
— Personnel — — File/Data Base Conversion
— Facilities — — Organization Changes
— Hardware & Software Selection & Acquisition /Installation
— Education & Training

Figure 4.1   SIRP Phases in Context

These objectives can be achieved through a set of allied phases: a business strategy definition phase, an information architecture phase, a technical architecture phase, a migration strategy phase and a tactical plans phase. These phases are shown graphically in Figure 4.1 along with their inputs and outputs.

4.2 THE SIRP PHASES

Phase 1—The Business Strategy Definition

The business strategy definition phase defines the corporate business strategies and describes the overall direction to be taken by the organization during a three- to five-year period. It defines:

- The organization's mission,
- Its objectives and goals,
- The critical success factors and how they should be measured,
- Strategic directions, and
- High-level information requirements.

The business strategy definition provides the basis for developing the information and technical architectures, and the migration strategy.

The MIS department only records information about the corporate business strategies. It is corporate management's responsibility to define and develop them. One exception is the MIS strategy or strategic information resource plan. (This SIRP is also known as the INFORMATICS strategy.) MIS management has the responsibility for defining and developing the SIRP strategy with senior management's participation.

From the corporate business viewpoint, the possible areas that could result in new strategic directions for the organization include:

- New businesses,
- New markets,
- Profit trends,
- New products and services,
- Current product stability, and
- Organizational philosophy.

Selection of each new strategy should result from:

- Definition of the organization's business views of this strategy in terms of the present, the immediate future and the distant future;
- Evaluation of the new products or services to be provided in terms of the industry structure and dynamics, and the company's strengths and weaknesses.

The SIRP project team could obtain information about the business strategies from sources such as the documented corporate business strategy, and interviews with the executive and line management. Most of the information is likely to be obtained from interviews. Interviews could be conducted with each executive separately or in discussion groups led by a facilitator. Tables 4.2 and 4.3 are examples of questions or issues that should be discussed. Table 4.2 is in two parts: The first should be completed with line management prior to meeting with the executive as it is quite detailed; these questions and answers are reviewed with the executive and the second part completed. The results should be documented and approved by the individual or group of individuals interviewed.

TABLE 4.2   Business Strategy Questionnaire

PART 1

The Business

• What is the company's business?
• What are your products?
• Who are your customers?
• Who are your prospective customers by product?
• Which areas of your business will be most critical in five years? Least critical? Why?
• On which markets do you focus?

  geographic
  industrial
  customer size
  retail/wholesale
  private/public/institutional sector

Mission and Objectives

• What is the corporate mission?
• What are the corporate objectives?
• What are your division objectives?
• Do you have problems in meeting objectives?
• Why are these problems not solved?
• What is needed to solve them?
• What are your current priorities?
• Do other areas need improvement?
• What is the value of these improvements?
• How are you measured?
• How do you measure your subordinates?

The Competition

• Do you know what your customers want?
• Do you know what your customers consider to be of value?
• Do you know your competitors?
• Do you know what they are offering your customers?
• How do your products and services compare with your competitors?
• What is your current position in the industry?
• Can you serve your customers better?
• Can your products and services be packaged better?
• Can your products and services be marketed better?
• Is your market changing? How?
• Are new products and services needed? Can you provide them?

TABLE 4.2   (Continued)

- Should existing products or services be modified or eliminated?
- What are your strengths and weaknesses?

PART 2

Critical Success Factors

(A critical success factor may be defined as anything that must be done properly or else a major objective may not be achieved.)

- List the critical success factors which impact your area of responsibility.
- How do you measure these CSFs?

Future Directions

- What major changes do you expect to occur that could affect the organization and your area of responsibility

    in the short term?
    in the long term?

- What type of information would you need when these changes occur

    in the short term?
    in the long term?

Office Automation

- What are your office automation objectives?
- What office automation functions should be provided? (See list of possible functions in Table 4.3.)
- Should the office automation organization be

    centralized?
    decentralized?
    under functional control?

- Should office automation be standardized

    across the organization?
    by department?
    by function?

  - Should office automation be implemented through

    universal standards?
    guidelines?
    recommended solutions?

Information Requirements

- What type of decisions do you make?
- What is the most useful information you currently receive?
- What critical information is not readily available?
- What new information do you require based on your replies to the preceding questions?
- Rate information currently received in terms of:

    type
    timeliness
    accuracy
    adequacy
    cost
    consistency
    ease of use

- What is your opinion about current information systems?

TABLE 4.2 *(Continued)*

• Do you have any concerns about the information management area?
Comments
• Do you have any other comments or concerns you would like to express?
Organization
• Provide an organization chart.
• What key functions does your department perform?
• Define your responsibilities.

Note: This questionnaire is divided into two parts: The first should be completed by first and second line management, and the second by executive management. The contents of the first part should be summarized before the executive interviews, and confirmed by the executive. Answers should be in *brief, point form only*.

TABLE 4.3   Office Automation Functions

Stand-alone Functions
Spreadsheet
Expert Systems
Graphics
Shared Functions
Word Processing
Electronic Mail
Messaging
Facsimile
Document Management and Electronic Filing
Management Support Applications (correspondence control, information logs, etc.)
Security
Time Management (calendar, meetings, etc.)
Mainframe/Mini: Data Download/Upload
Data Base/File Access
Query Languages
Graphics
Decision Support Systems
Distributed Processing
Shared Data Bases
Communications
Local Area Networks
Digital PBXs
Video Transmission
Long Distance Networks

The business strategy definition should provide a clear understanding of the business, the strategic directions the organization plans to follow, the primary information issues, and the critical success factors. This information then forms the basis for developing the information and technical architectures.

Phase 2—The Information Architecture

The information architecture encompasses both the data and application architectures. This is illustrated in Figure 4.2. The data and application architectures are developed to support the functions performed in the organization. Analysis of these functions leads to the identification of the data entities and business applications. The entities are modeled at different levels providing entity-relationship diagrams and subject data bases. The subject data bases and the business applications are related in that certain applications usually create or update data, while others only use data. Later, the subject data bases are expanded to become records with keys and data attributes, which then become the basis for physical data base design.

The information architecture is the basis for information resource management, which is discussed in the next chapter. It is also the basis for the design of the technical architecture in the next phase.

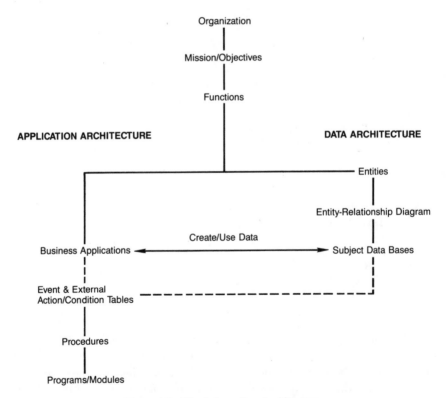

Figure 4.2 The Information Architecture

Functions performed by the organization are identified by interviews with senior user management and their representatives. The functions are independent of the organization structure, although an understanding of this structure provides a starting point for function analysis. Examples of high-level functions are marketing, manufacturing and distribution. This subject is examined in more depth in the next chapter.

Entities are identified that support the functions. Examples of entities are products, customers, suppliers and warehouses. A few of these high-level entities are the essence of the business. When related, they provide the crown (highest level entity-relationship diagram) of the corporate data model.

Modeling the entities to indicate how they relate to one another provides the corporate entity-relationship diagram. An average business may have 400 to 500 entities defined at different hierarchical levels. How many of these entities should be identified and modeled to produce an entity-relationship diagram that effectively reflects the business? The entity-relationship diagram reflects the corporate or high-level view of the business; hence, two or at the most three function levels should be analyzed.

Computer systems consist of sets of instructions which create or modify data. For purposes of organization and control, business functions are grouped together in the form of business applications, which in turn become physical application systems. The data that are processed are stored in files or data bases. To arrive at these results, we need to define logical function sets or business applications, and logical data groups or subject data bases. We do this keeping in mind that certain applications primarily create or update data, specifically subject data bases, while other applications only use or access the data.

Once we have defined the business applications and the subject data bases and shown the associations between them, we have defined the basic information architecture. As mentioned earlier, the information architecture forms the basis for defining the technical architecture in the next phase. If management had defined the SIRP's scope to include a fairly accurate assessment of computer processing and data storage needs in the technical architecture phase, then more work would be required in this phase than a mere extrapolation of existing processing and storage capacities.

This additional effort includes work that would usually be done during the tactical and operational planning levels. The information needed is a reflection of record content, such as their attributes, the numbers of records, the accesses to the records in the data base, and the processing involved in the updating of the data. To do this in detail would not fit the definition of "strategic planning." But some expansion of data, normalization of the expanded data, estimates of numbers of records, estimated data accesses and function processing must be done. Finally, a first pass is made to name the critical business applications and to set priorities for their development.

Phase 3—The Technical Architecture

The design of the technical architecture provides the foundation for the future technical environment. It is planned, designed and implemented in terms of the entire information architecture and not in terms of specific application needs.

The technical architecture is an overview of the hardware, software, communications and office automation environment required to support the information architecture. Development of the technical architecture will probably need assistance from the technical support staff in the MIS department. It is emphasized that the architecture is conceptual and should not entail the naming of specific products. The different business strategies the organization has defined should serve as the basis for the architecture.

The business may be located in one spot or consist of branches or warehouses distributed over a wide area. Control may be centralized or distributed. An analysis is needed to determine where the different functions are performed so that a decision can be reached on whether to centralize or decentralize the processing and storage of data. This decision may also be influenced by management policies determined during the business strategy definition phase.

If processing functions and data are to be distributed, the analysis should define which business functions and which data will be duplicated, and what type of data abstraction will be needed at the central location. It should also include where and when the data need to be updated periodically or instantly.

Computer support will be needed to execute the business functions and store the data. An analysis should be done to identify the different computer functions that may be needed such as multi-tasking, network support, multiple screen handling, data base management and inquiry, data dictionary or encyclopedia, and so forth. These functions should provide information to subsequently identify the types (mainframe, mini and micro) and capacities of the different computers, along with storage capacities needed at the different locations. Other input to this analysis could include the data usage analysis that may have been conducted during the information architecture phase.

Office automation includes functions such as electronic mail, word processing, expert and decision support systems, spreadsheets, graphics, and so forth. If office automation had been included in the SIRP scope, a high-level study should be conducted to determine office automation hardware, software and communications requirements. Based on all of these stated functions and their locations, the mix of computer types and capacities is defined.

To link the different computers, communications support (voice, digital, networks, etc.) is needed. This is defined in gross terms and expanded in detail during the tactical planning stage.

TABLE 4.4   Technical Architecture Outputs

Table linking applications to subject data bases
Data usage analysis
Table relating functions to locations
Table linking subject data bases to locations
Table linking subject data bases, update locations and response times
Table linking computing functions and applications
Table linking computing functions and memory
Table linking applications and storage
Table linking memory and locations
Table linking storage and locations
Office automation report
List of software requirements
List of communications support requirements
List of analyst/programmer support needs
List of possible building modifications

Computer software is needed to support the business and office automation functions. At the strategic planning level, this software identification is restricted to a high-level view by type and is expanded in detail during the tactical planning stage. If the scope had included hardware and software to make the analysts and programmers more effective, such as an analyst/programmer's workbench, these requirements should be added to the hardware and software needs.

The hardware, software and network needs may exceed the present building area, weight limits and ducting capacities. These needs will have to be identified and considered in the future plans, as they will probably have a major impact on decisions made.

The different analyses provide a series of outputs. Table 4.4 is a comprehensive list of these outputs.

Phase 4—The Migration Strategy

The migration strategy is intended to provide the best approach to move from the present to the future. It encompasses all aspects of the information and the technical architectures, and evaluates the present environment.

To be able to move from the present application and technical environments to the planned goals defined in the information and technical architectures, one must have a thorough understanding of what exists today. These are major tasks. However, one could spend much more time and effort than is necessary on these tasks attempting to create documentation that either does not exist or to update documentation that is inadequate.

In terms of migration, four areas need to be assessed. These are the current applications in production, the current technical environment, and the MIS and user organizations.

To assess the current applications, all existing production systems are listed. This information may be found in the systems documentation library, program libraries and computer operations documentation. At this time, where information on the systems and their files is located is noted. In most organizations it should not be too difficult to list all current production systems. In some very large companies, this may present a problem and may require considerable effort to identify them.

The production files associated with each application system are reviewed. The data stored in each file and their data structure are defined. In an ideal organization, all information on application systems, files and data structures would be found in the data dictionary/directory. This is usually not the case. Most often it requires a major project to properly identify and correlate all the information about files and data. If this information is not readily available at this stage, it is sufficient to name the files and the data found in them without being specific about data redundancy, inconsistency and incompatibility. This analysis should be done in detail during the tactical planning stage.

The documentation of each application and its strengths and weaknesses are reviewed with the users and the staff responsible for maintaining the application to determine whether the application should remain unchanged, be modified or replaced. Certain applications may be classed as "to be retained" even though they may be prime choices for replacement because of poor data structures or messy program code. This could result from circumstances beyond the control of the company such as use of a common airline reservation system or the commitment to and investment in a particular vendor package. In these circumstances, it may be necessary during the tactical and operational stages to design ideal data structures and applications and use this design to influence change when the opportunity arises in the future.

The current applications are compared with the proposed applications and a list of applications for development or modification is prepared. These applications should form the bulk of the development work to be done during the period covered by the SIRP.

Priorities for new systems development and for systems modification based on the migration strategy and users' needs are established. This application development and modification will occur during the operational planning stage, and will be based on development and expansion of the functions and the corporate entity-relationship diagram during the tactical planning stage.

An inventory of current hardware, software, communications and office automation products in use is created if none exists. This inventory is compared with the hardware, software, communications and office automation needs specified, and inventories of products to be replaced and to be acquired are prepared. This evaluation is intended to provide a realistic appraisal of the current products in use in terms of the technical architecture specified.

Finally, an organizational review is conducted to determine:

- The availability of MIS resources (people);
- The existence, strengths, and weaknesses of the data administration function;
- The existence, strengths, and weaknesses of the systems development methodologies in use;
- Staff needs for education; and
- The user department's capacity for implementing application systems.

This assessment could result in organizational changes, education being planned, and so forth.

Long-range plans are developed for:

- Proposed technical architecture design, development, and installation (hardware, software and communications);
- Logical data base development;
- Physical data base design;
- Application systems development or modification;
- Office automation; and
- MIS and user organization and administration.

It is emphasized that these are migration plans and *not* detailed project plans. It is more important to define how the pieces fit together than it is to precisely define projects with resources and schedules.

MIS Planning Options

The migration strategy will be influenced by the strategic business plan in effect for the corporation, the degree of dissatisfaction with the existing MIS services, and the type of individuals on the steering committee and in charge of MIS. The resulting migration strategy may include high, moderate and low risks. Table 4.5 examines the risk levels and relates them to the key areas affected, such as data, new and current applications, technology, investment and service levels.

The high risk level emphasizes doing as much as possible at once while freezing development and enhancement. This results in reduced service to the users over the short term and also tempts fate by assuming that every-

TABLE 4.5 MIS Planning Options

High Risk/Short Term (immediate results)	Medium Risk/ Business Critical Success Factors (CSFs) and Objectives (mid-term results)	Low Risk/Long Term (delayed results)
DATA		
Corporate E-R Model Subject data bases (SDBs) parallel design	Corporate E-R Model Subject data bases (SDBs) parallel and sequential design based on CSFs and objectives	Corporate E-R Model Subject data bases (SDBs) sequential design developed in areas of least impact to gain experience
Convert current files to new SDB environment immediately	Convert current files to new SDB environment synchronized with application development	Convert current files to new SDB environment and build bridges between present files and future data bases
APPLICATIONS—NEW		
Develop major applications in parallel with subject data bases	Develop major applications as dictated by CSFs and objectives	Develop pilot systems followed by minor applications to gain experience
APPLICATIONS—CURRENT		
Maintain systems and freeze updates	Maintain systems and enhance those systems not under redevelopment	Maintain and enhance all systems while new systems under development
Completely replace with new systems	Completely replace with new systems	Build on existing systems
TECHNOLOGY		
Intensive program to install all new hardware, software and networks over a short period	Install hardware, software and networks synchronized with new application development	Install hardware, software and networks in parallel with pilot systems and minor applications to become familiar with products
INVESTMENT		
High investment on development and technology, and low system maintenance cost	Moderate investment on development and technology, and moderate maintenance cost	Low investment on development and technology, and high maintenance cost
SERVICE LEVELS		
Considerably reduced service until new systems implemented	Reduced service until new systems implemented	Current service maintained

thing that is acquired, developed and installed will work as planned. The gamble may pay off with MIS management becoming heros, or may fail with new management being brought in to solve the ensuing problems.

The moderate risk level ties in with the business's objectives and critical success factors (CSFs) and is an orderly migration. There is a small price to be paid though with some loss of existing service levels to the users.

The low risk level continues to provide current service levels. Migration can be slow and take much longer than with the moderate approach.

Is there a universal solution? Apparently not, for no two organizations are alike. What is likely to occur is that the migration strategy will include aspects from all three levels of risk.

Phase 5—The Tactical Plans

Projects to implement the migration strategy should be set up for a minimum of six months and a maximum of two years. These projects should have approved priorities, budgets and schedules. At periodic intervals, possibly every six months, the migration strategy should be reviewed and the tactical plans updated. This would also be an appropriate time to review the project's status and establish new projects.

It may be assumed that only projects of fixed duration comprise the tactical plans. In fact, they also include ongoing functions, such as data administration. These projects and functions can be grouped under the business, the data, the applications and the technical environment.

From the business viewpoint, the plans should include expansion of the business functions, the definition of policies for the development and use of application system development methodologies, and organizational change in the MIS department. Provision should be made in the organization for new functions such as information resource management, the information center, communications, education, strategic planning and quality assurance.

From the data perspective, logical data bases should be developed and maintained. This involves expansion of the subject data bases in terms of the detailed business functions, comparison of these subject data bases with existing files and documents, normalization of data, and data distribution analysis.

In terms of the applications, physical applications must be defined from the logical applications named in the SIRP. These definitions should be in sufficient detail to enable each application to be developed. The definitions should include the type of system, such as interactive, batch, online work files with overnight batch update, and centralized or distributed processing and storage. They should also include the mix of hardware, software and communications involved, and how they relate to the overall plans for the technical environment.

Tactical plans for the technical environment include the complete specification and selection of all hardware, software and communications defined in the SIRP. These should also include office automation needs that may have been defined. Because technology is changing very rapidly, these plans must be flexible and adjusted for new products that may not have been available when the initial SIRP was developed. Further, the new knowledge may even involve rethinking of the strategic plans for the technical environment.

5
Information Resource Management (IRM)—The Basics

STRIPE PHASES

SP2   The Information Architecture
TP1   Function Expansion
TP2   Logical Data Base Design
TP3   Physical Application Definition
OP2   Business System Specification
OP3   Procedure Design

In this chapter, we introduce information resource management and some of the techniques used with it. In Chapters 6, 7 and 8, we describe IRM in terms of the STRIPE strategic, tactical and operational activities. Table 5.1 highlights the IRM outputs on the STRIPE matrix.

Information resource management is the management of all enterprise data and the business applications which process those data. Information resource management includes conceptual or logical system design to the extent that data are analyzed to define the logic associated with data update and extraction. Physical system design is treated as part of the application design and development process and is discussed in Chapters 9 through 12.

TABLE 5.1 The STRIPE Matrix Highlighting the Information Resource Management Outputs

	Business	Data	Application	Technical Environment	Type of Plan
STRATEGIC PLANNING	SP1 Business Strategy: Mission, Objectives and Goals, Strategic Directions, Critical Success Factors (CSFs), Major Information Requirements; SP2 Major Functions (Processes); SP4 User and MIS Department Evaluation; SP4 Proposed Organizations	SP2 Data Architecture: Primary Entities, Crown, E-R Diagram, Subject Data Bases	SP2 Application Architecture: Business Applications; SP4 Current Application Evaluation	SP3 Technical Architecture: Function Distribution, Computers and Peripherals, Data Distribution, Communications, Software (DBMS, Dictionary, Security), Office Automation; SP4 Evaluation of Current Hardware/Software, Communications and Office Automation	SP4 Migration Plan: Major Projects over a 3–5 year period
TACTICAL PLANNING	TP1 Function Expansion; TP1 ASDM Policy; TP1 Organization Change: IRM Function, Education Function, Strategic Planning Function, Quality Assurance	TP2 Logical Data Bases: Entity Expansion, Current Files/Documents Comparison, Data Normalization, Data Distribution	TP3 Physical Application Definition	TP4 Hardware/Software, Communications/ Office Automation Specifications; TP5 Selection of: Computers, etc., Communications Equipment, Software, Office Automation Equipment and Software	SP5 Budget Year Plan: (or similar period); Prioritized Projects scheduled and resourced
OPERATIONAL PLANNING	OP2 Business System Specifications: Activity Level Functions, Output Requirements, Output Design; OP9 System Implementation: Manual Procedures, D.P. Operations Procedures, Education; OP7 System Test: Testing; OP10 System Review: Business Needs, Operating Efficiency	OP4 Physical Data Base Design: Activity Level, Data Volumes, Data Accesses, Physical Data Bases, Physical DB Access Modules; OP7 Testing; OP9 File Conversion	OP3 Procedure Design: Event and External Action/Condition Analysis, Embryonic Procedures, Menu Hierarchies, Input Screens and Forms, File Update Logic, Output Logic; OP5 Procedure Expansion:; OP6 System Construction: Physical Procedures; OP8 Package Acquisition; OP7 System Test: Testing; OP9 Production Libraries	OP11 Product Implementation: Product Acquisition, Product Installation, Product Conversion, Product Testing	OP1 Individual Project Plans

The basis for information resource management is the information architecture. The information architecture is made up of the data and application architectures. Refer to Figure 4.2 for a graphic illustration of the relationships between the architectures. The information architecture provides a total view of the organization's information needs and how they are met. These information needs stem from the organization's mission and objectives, and the major functions it performs to meet those objectives. Analysis of the functions in terms of the business rules and policies provides us with the application and data architectures.

Regardless of the strategies and techniques used to obtain them, the end products to meet the users' information processing needs are a set of application systems and a set of data files or data bases. The application systems are well designed if they meet the business function's information requirements, are easy to use and to operate, are easy to maintain (for example, to correct problems that occur), and are easily modified or enhanced. The data files are well designed if they reflect the organization's business without data inconsistency, redundancy and incompatibility.

Data inconsistency occurs when multiple applications use the same data but with different names and shades of meaning. Data redundancy occurs when the same data are stored in different files, with the result that file updates do not occur simultaneously and information extracted from different files for different purposes contain different data. Data incompatibility occurs when data are structured differently in different files requiring complex interfaces to pass data to and fro.

In the data architecture, identification and analysis of the business functions provide the real-world entities with which the organization is concerned. These entities are expanded and related to one another using entity-relationship (E-R) diagrams. The E-R diagrams, in turn, are divided into entity sets or subject data bases. The subject data bases are expanded to records with keys and data attributes.

In the application architecture, functions are grouped or subdivided into business applications. These business applications either create data (add, delete or modify records) or use data (read records). Subject data bases are linked to application systems which create and/or use their data.

Every data change (function event) is caused by an action or condition that occurs in the world outside of the computer system. "Data create" (update) type applications are developed through analysis of the records in related subject data bases in terms of function events, actions and conditions. "Data use" type applications are developed in terms of outputs (reports, screens, and so forth) obtained by reading (accessing) data in files. Of course, most "data create" type applications also contain "data use" type functions.

External actions/conditions provide for the groupings of function events into embryonic procedures. These embryonic procedures, in turn, are expanded to include data validation, algorithmic logic, external interface and output production functions. The expanded procedures are grouped into modules and programs and physically coded. All these processes are examined in detail in following chapters.

If information resource management is not applied in an organization, the organization will continue to operate with application systems designed as separate entities with no shared data. Problems with data inconsistency, redundancy and incompatibility will become worse over time with resulting high costs in data processing and system maintenance.

In another scenario, an organization may wish to introduce information resource management in conjunction with the development of a large system. This is a very practical approach and reduces the scope of the problem to the system boundaries. Later, as more systems are added to the information architecture, the entity-relationship model should grow into the corporate model. This bottom-up approach is not as effective as the top-down approach as it does not attempt to meet the information needs of the corporation as a whole, but builds them up in terms of specific problem areas.

The following case study describes a chain of hotels and is used to illustrate the examples found in the text. Appendix A is a comprehensive model of the different outputs discussed throughout the book. The tables in the text and Appendix A are cross-referenced so that the reader can move from the limited example in the text to the complete example in the appendix.

5.1 CASE STUDY

The Vacation Hotel chain has hotels in Canada and the United States. Each hotel is a franchise and operates as a separate company. However, the corporate office provides certain centralized services, such as advertising and reservations, and also sets performance standards which are closely monitored. Nonadherence to these standards could result in warnings being issued and cancellation of the franchise.

The first Vacation Hotel was opened in 1980. There is now a total of 55 hotels. Computerization of systems has been limited to accounting functions such as customer billing. Reservations are done manually both in the corporate office and in the individual hotels. The company has decided to modernize its administration and has undertaken the development of a strategic business plan to be implemented over five years. This plan includes definition of the mission statement, corporate objectives, critical success factors, specific management information requirements and future plans. These are summarized in the following pages.

The business plan also calls for the development of a strategic information resource plan for the management services division to define the business applications and the data required to process them, the hardware and software including communications' needs, a migration strategy and tactical plans to move from the present situation to the planned future. Now let's look at the case study business plan.

Vacation Hotel Mission Statement

The Vacation Hotel chain's mission is to satisfy a market requirement for high-quality hotel accommodation at reasonable prices supported by high-quality service.

The market consists of two groups of people, that is, business and tourist. The hotels are advertised in travel magazines and television.

CORPORATE OBJECTIVES

1. To rank within the first ten hotel chains in North America within five years in terms of numbers of hotels and in service.

2. To achieve an average annual occupancy of 80 percent of available bedrooms within two years.

3. To achieve an average annual occupancy of 60 percent of meeting and banquet rooms within two years.

CRITICAL SUCCESS FACTORS

1. To provide top quality (in terms of specific standards) accommodation, restaurant services, meeting, banquet and convention facilities.

2. To provide these services at competitive prices.

3. To provide centralized and local reservation facilities with immediate response capability to satisfy customer needs.

MANAGEMENT INFORMATION REQUIREMENTS

1. To access data on reservations, occupancy, quality of service, cash flow, and so on both centrally and by individual hotel.

FUTURE PLANS

1. The hotel chain is to be increased to 75 hotels over the next five years and the locations will be expanded to include the West Indies.

The Strategic Information Resource Plan

Following development of the business strategy, an information model must be developed which includes an entity-relationship diagram and the business applications the company needs. This model will then be used as the foundation for building computerized application systems, acquiring appropriate hardware, software and communications, and migrating from the present way of operating to the planned future way.

Primary Functions of the Organization

These are defined at both the corporate and individual hotel levels. The two functions which are common are financial services and administration.

1 CORPORATE LEVEL

Financial Services

Marketing

Hotel Construction

Franchise Sales

Franchise Management

Room Reservations and Occupancy

Head Office Administration

2 HOTEL LEVEL

Financial Services

Room Reservations and Occupancy

Equipment Management

Recreation

Shop Management

Restaurant Management

External Services

Hotel Administration

5.2 THE ANSI/SPARC THREE-SCHEMA DATA ARCHITECTURE (1)

The ANSI/SPARC committee has defined a three-schema data architecture as a standard for data modeling. The schemas are the external or user view, the conceptual or logical view and the internal view of the physical data base or file design. This concept is illustrated in Figure 5.1.

The external schema is any user view or subschema of the overall conceptual schema of the business, business function or system being modeled. A user view may be a report, a screen, a data flow or a programming requirement. In fact, it could be any related set of data needed for a particular purpose.

The conceptual schema is the overall view of data of the area being

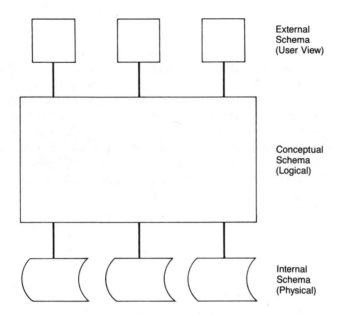

Figure 5.1   The ANSI/SPARC Three-Schema Data Architecture

modeled. This logical schema can be derived from a top-down understanding of the business or synthesized from all the external user views. In this chapter, we discuss synthesis under the heading of "Canonical Synthesis," that is, synthesis based on a set of rules and directed at producing a canonical data model. In Chapter 6, we discuss the top-down approach.

The data architecture is the basis or foundation for developing the conceptual schema. The internal schema is the physical representation of the conceptual schema in the form of physical files or data bases. All three schema levels can be modeled using entity-relationship diagrams.

5.3 ENTITY-RELATIONSHIP DIAGRAMS

The entity-relationship diagram is intended to model the business practices and policies through identification of entities and their relationships to one another based on the rules of the business. These diagrams do not illustrate processes or flows of data. They meet two objectives: The first is to provide a high-level view of the business so that management, users and system design staff can reach agreement on the view, and to use this view to design data bases and application systems to carry out the different business functions. The second is to provide the foundation for the different data bases that must be designed to support the applications without data inconsistency, incompatibility and redundancy.

The essential components of the E-R diagram are entities and associations, or relationships between entities. These relationships are quantitative, that is, one-to-one, one-to-many or many-to-many; and verbal such as "belongs to" and "is a product of." Sometimes included in the E-R diagrams are indicators of optional and mandatory relationships.

Entity-relationship diagrams have only three types of entities: independent entities, dependent entities and relationship entities. An independent entity has no parent entity and its key is a single data element. For example, "Hotel" is an independent entity because it can be identified uniquely by a data element such as "Hotel Name" or "Hotel Identification Number." (Those familiar with hierarchical data base design would recognize an independent entity as a "root" or entry point).

```
HOTEL (Hotel, Address, Number of Rooms)
```

A dependent entity has a parent entity and its key includes the parent entity key, for example, "Hotel Room."

```
HOTEL ROOM (Hotel, Room Number, Room Rate)
```

A relationship entity links two (or more) entities and includes the keys from these entities. However, these keys may or may not be part of the relationship entity key. Consider the following example:

```
BANQUET ROOMS/     BANQUET ROOM RESERVATION (Hotel, Room
CUSTOMER           No., Customer Id., Reserv. Ref. Arrival Date, Time
Relationship       of Day, Departure Date, Payment Method, No. At-
                   tending, Table Type, Coffee Break, Lunch, Dinner)
```

In this example, "Banquet Room" is linked to "Customer." Here the "Banquet Room" key and the "Customer" key together form part of the "Banquet Room Reservation" key. If a unique number could be given to the "Reservation Reference," then "Hotel," "Room Number" and "Customer Identification" could become attribute foreign keys.

Many techniques for drawing E-R diagrams are advocated by different authorities. Most of these are based on two models, Martin's (2, 3) and Chen's (4) which are networks. I have developed an approach based on natural entity families which both analyst and user easily learn and which convert very simply to canonical (normalized) data models. The normalized models may be converted to physical data base management systems which can be hierarchical, network or relational. All three techniques are described in the following pages.

The James Martin Technique (2)

Figure 5.2 is an example of a James Martin E-R diagram. The entities are linked by single- and double-headed arrows. For example, a single location (city) can have many hotels in it. The square boxes, such as "Charge" and "Service," are special entities called intersection data (also called relationships entities) because they provide a link between independent entities which have a one-to-many or many-to-many association. For example, a hotel can have many customers and a customer can stay in many hotels.

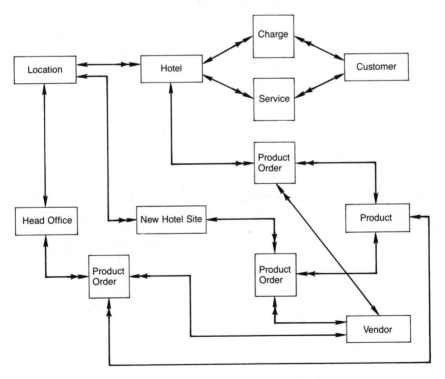

Figure 5.2 Martin Entity-Relationship Diagram

A more complex example is the product order entity which is shown in three different positions. Let's examine one of them, for example, the one linking "Hotel," "Product" and "Vendor." "Hotel" and "Product," "Hotel" and "Vendor," and "Vendor" and "Product" each have many-to-many relationships. The proper term for the intersection or relationship entity linking them would be "Hotel–Vendor–Product Order." Similarly, we would have "New Hotel Site–Vendor–Product Order" and "Head Office–Vendor–Product Order." But we know that the same product order is commonly used in any particular organization. So, later when product order is expanded into a record, "Hotel," "New Hotel Site" and "Head Office" will be replaced by a generic term such as *site* or *department*.

James Martin does not advocate the identification of all entities during the E-R diagramming stage, as the E-R diagram is a very high-level view of the business. Further entities and intersection data are added when subject data bases are modeled in detail.

The Peter Chen Technique (4)

Figure 5.3 illustrates Peter Chen's approach to drawing E-R diagrams. The entities are represented by rectangles and are related through diamonds. He

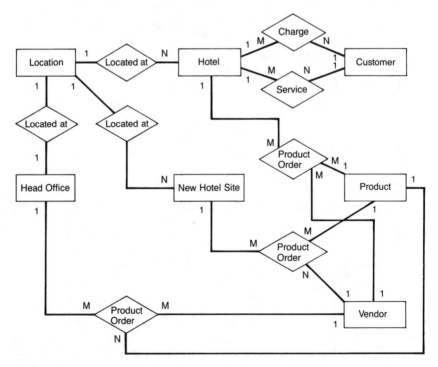

Figure 5.3   Chen Entity-Relationship Diagram

uses l, M and N to indicate the one-to-many and many-to-many relationships. Some relationships, such as "Located At" are descriptive while others can become entities. Examples of these relationship entities are "Charge," "Service" and "Product Order." The naming of "Product Order" was discussed in the James Martin technique. The same argument applies here.

The Denis Connor "STRIPE" Technique

Both Martin's and Chen's techniques are networks. The problem with networks is that lines crisscross even in the simplest of situations, with the result that the diagram looks like a bowl of spaghetti. When one has to diagram complex situations where many-to-many relationships abound and where one relationship entity associates several entities, such as a bill of lading, the diagrams can become very messy and hard to understand.

An approach which makes use of natural entity families, in the fact that they consist of independent, dependent or relationship entities, permits the diagramming to be done in terms of homogeneous sets. Each family has a single independent entity and can have multiple dependent entities and multiple relationship entities. The relationship entities will occur as "children" or dependent entities in each family to which they relate. These relationship entities are redundant on the diagram, but are defined only once in the data dictionary.

Each family or leg of a family can be drawn on a separate page. This eliminates the crossing of lines and provides a means of limiting the number of items drawn on any one page. The disadvantage of this approach is that relationship entities are replicated in different families when they are drawn manually.

It should be emphasized that this data modeling technique provides the same information as any other entity-relationship diagramming technique, and can be converted into a network model using appropriate computer software. Here, each entity family can be treated as subschema or user view.

Figure 5.4 contains four separate families: "Location," "Vendor," "Product" and "Customer." Each family is complete and as a result the entity relationships are repeated in each family. These are highlighted by ellipses. Also shown are pointers to the associated entities, for example, "To Customer" and "To Vendor." These pointers need not be shown on the diagram but should be included in the dictionary or encyclopedia used to record the data diagrammed.

Other advantages of the STRIPE modeling technique are:

• Every independent entity can be expanded into a family independent of all other independent entities.

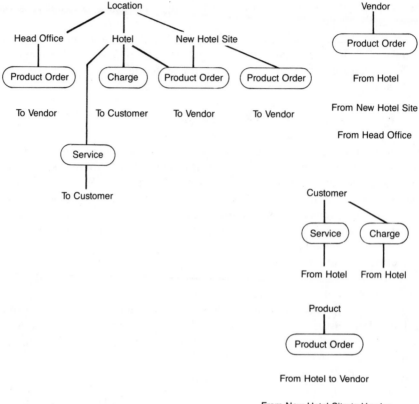

Figure 5.4   Connor "STRIPE" Entity-Relationship Diagram

- The initial identification of relationships or associations is restricted to parent-child relationships.
- Each family can be normalized independent of the other families.
- The model tends to be canonical, that is, completely normalized. (See Section 5.4).
- Relationship entities need to be recorded in the dictionary only once, but may have additional attributes and foreign keys added as further entities are expanded into families.
- The model easily converts into a network using appropriate software.

This modeling technique is used to develop the detailed data models described in this text.

5.4 NORMALIZATION

Before we discuss the detailed design and development of the information architecture, we should understand how data are simplified and organized to support data update, modification, deletion and access. This is done using a process called normalization. Normalization is a term coined by E. F. Codd (5). The schema which results from normalization is called a canonical schema.

Normalized records are always flat files or tables called relations. These relations can then be used in a relational data base management system, or adapted for use in both hierarchical and network data base management systems.

Normalization greatly increases the number of records defined in a data base over the initial definition of entities in the E-R diagram. Needless to say, this increases the file accesses or inputs/outputs by the programs. Whether a physical data base is a direct reflection or a major modification of a canonical data model will depend on several factors such as the type of data base management system in use and its machine efficiency, required response times, ease of data base update and report preparation.

A normalized record is defined as a record in which every descriptor (data attribute) is a fact about the whole key and nothing but the key. The normalization process removes the interdependencies among data attributes.

Normalization has three basic forms or steps termed first, second and third normal form. Other normal forms are Boyce-Codd, fourth and fifth normal forms. A final normalization aid we will discuss is the use of cross-indices which eliminate unnecessary replication of data.

First, Second and Third Normal Form

In first normal form, all repeating groups are converted to individual records. Second normal form only applies to records with concatenated keys. In these records, data attributes not dependent on all elements of the key are converted to individual records. In third normal form, data attributes which are dependent on other data attributes and not on the key are converted to individual records.

Figure 5.5 illustrates the use of first, second and third normal forms using a customer invoice as an example. In the customer invoice, the unnormalized record has data on the customer, the customer's invoices and the invoice line items. Proceeding to first normal form, we have three records which form a hierarchy. These are the customer, the invoice and the invoice line item. The key for the customer record is "Customer Id."; for the invoice, it is "Customer Id." and "Invoice Number"; and for invoice line

UN-NORMALIZED

CUSTOMER ID.
Customer Name
Customer Address
FIRST LEVEL REPEAT
Invoice Number
Invoice Date
Invoice Total
SECOND LEVEL REPEAT
Line Number
Product Description
Product Quantity
Unit Price
Amount

1ST NORMAL FORM

CUSTOMER ID.
Customer Name
Customer Address

CUSTOMER ID.
INVOICE NUMBER
Invoice Date
Invoice Total

CUSTOMER ID.
INVOICE NUMBER
LINE NUMBER
Product Description
Product Quantity
Unit Price
Amount

2ND NORMAL FORM

INVOICE NUMBER
Invoice Date
Invoice Total
Customer Id.

INVOICE NUMBER
LINE NUMBER
Product Description
Product Quantity
Unit Price
Amount

3RD NORMAL FORM

INVOICE NUMBER
LINE NUMBER
Product Id.
Product Quantity
Amount

PRODUCT ID.
Product Description
Unit Price

Figure 5.5   First, Second and Third Normal Form (normalized records in boxes).

item, it is "Customer Id.," "Invoice Number" and "Line Number." These three records are flat tables and hence are in first normal form.

Reviewing these records, we note that invoice can be identified by a unique identifier, for example, "Invoice Number" and, in invoice and invoice line item we find that the data attributes are not dependent on "Customer Id.," so we remove it from their keys. But to show the association between customer and invoice, we include "Customer Id." as a foreign key in "Invoice." Invoice line item is a child of invoice. This dependency is shown through "Invoice Number" in the invoice line item key. Invoice and Invoice line item are now in second normal form.

Once again reviewing these records, we find in the invoice line item record that unit price is dependent on product description, another attribute, and not on the key. This leads us to create a new record called "Product" and introduce a new key called "Product Id." "Product Id." also becomes a foreign key data attribute of the invoice line item record to provide the link between the product and invoice line item. Invoice line item and product are now in third normal form. The end result is four records: "Customer," "Invoice," "Invoice Line Item" and "Product."

In most circumstances, these three levels of normalization should be sufficient. It has been shown that even when records are in third normal form, structure errors and data redundancies can occur. The following discussion covers these situations.

Boyce-Codd Normal Form

Boyce and Codd found that though records may be in third normal form, a situation could occur where a data element forming part of the key may be dependent on an attribute. Consider the following record, Product Territory:

Product, Territory, Salesman

This record describes the territory covered by a salesman for a particular product. Sometimes, salesmen have fixed territories even though the products they sell may change. In this type of situation, territory is dependent on salesman and we have a Boyce-Codd normalization error. Should the salesman change, the product territory record would have to be deleted and a new record established. The solution to this problem is to create two records:

Product, Salesman and
Salesman, Territory

The error occurred because of an incorrect understanding of the data element "Territory" and its dependence on "Salesman."

Fourth Normal Form

Fourth normal form covers the occurrence of multivalued dependencies. In fourth normal form, a record type should not contain two or more independent multivalued facts about an entity. Consider the following example,

"Aircraft" which is identified by a key consisting of "Aircraft–Airline–Part." Here, the aircraft manufacturer wishes to maintain a record of all parts used in any aircraft by any airline. The "Aircraft" entity can have many independent values for "Airline" and "Part."

Considerable redundancy will occur because a new record must be created for a part every time an airline buys a particular aircraft. This redundancy is eliminated by establishing two records:

Aircraft, Airline and
Aircraft, Part

Fifth Normal Form

Fifth normal form occurs when relational projection creates new records and these records cannot be synthesized to produce the original record. The possibility of this type of situation occurring is rare. The following example illustrates fifth normal form:

Certain independent insurance agents are authorized to sell specific types of insurance for specific companies.

Relation 1

Agent	Insurance Company	Insurance Type
Jones	Company A	Auto
Smith	Company A	Home
Brown	Company B	Life
Black	Company B	Auto

Projection provides Relations 2&3

Relation 2

Agent	Insurance Company
Jones	Company A
Smith	Company A
Brown	Company B
Black	Company B

Relation 3

Insurance Company	Insurance Type
Company A	Auto
Company A	Home
Company B	Life
Company B	Auto

Joining Relations 2&3 with Insurance Company in common gives Relation 4.

Relation 4

Agent	Insurance Company	Insurance Type
Jones	Company A	Auto
Jones	Company A	Home
Smith	Company A	Auto
Smith	Company A	Home
Brown	Company B	Life
Brown	Company B	Auto
Black	Company B	Life
Black	Company B	Auto

But from Relation 1 we know that Jones is not authorized to sell home insurance for Company A, Smith is not authorized to sell auto insurance for Company A, and so on.

In fifth normal form situations, the multivalued attributes are highly dependent and cannot be separated. Hence, they must make up the key together.

Cross-Indices

The preceding examples illustrate records as cross-indices where the entire record is made up of the key. These indices are very effective in reducing data redundancy. Consider the following example: Aircraft use a variety of parts and each part could be used on many aircraft. The relationship "Aircraft, Part" permits all data on aircraft and parts to be maintained independently. Without this relationship, every "Aircraft" record would have a multivalued dependency with "Part" as a foreign key, and every "Part" record would contain a multivalued dependency with "Aircraft" as a foreign key.

Normalization and the "STRIPE" E-R Model

We mentioned earlier that the Denis Connor STRIPE E-R modeling technique tended to produce a completely normalized data model. Let us apply the rules of normalization to the technique.

First normal form eliminates repeating groups. The STRIPE independent and dependent entities achieve the same result.

Second normal form requires all attributes to be dependent on the whole key. Since each dependent entity is clearly defined within the data hierarchy, the key is dependent on the parents and the entity itself. The attributes are then defined to describe the particular entity and nothing external to it.

Third normal form eliminates attribute-to-attribute dependencies. Attributes being described by other attributes are generally keys of independent entities or foreign keys. If this should happen, the occurrence of the foreign key automatically indicates a new entity to be defined, if it has not already been defined elsewhere in the model.

Boyce-Codd normal form, where a key could be dependent on an attribute, should not occur as such attributes can only be foreign keys indicating a new entity.

Fourth and fifth normal form cover the occurrence of multivalued dependencies. These multivalued facts are generally foreign keys occurring in relationship entities. If these facts are independent of one another, new entities should be defined. If they are not, they may remain in the relationship entity.

5.5 CANONICAL SYNTHESIS

In Chapters 6 and 7, we will cover the development of entity-relationship and detailed data models using a top-down approach. James Martin in several of his text books including *Computer Data-Base Organization* (3) describes a bottom-up approach called canonical synthesis. Canonical synthesis is the development of a canonical schema through the sequential normalization of a series of user views (subschemas). These user views are the external views of data defined in the ANSI/SPARC (1) model. Stated in another way, it is based on the data requirements of the inputs and outputs. It is assumed that a stable data model designed in this way can be updated as the need for additional data requirements arises.

The principle followed in the process is very simple. Take the first user view and normalize it producing a data model. Then take the second user view and superimpose it over the first. Normalize this model. Then take the third and do the same until all the user views are incorporated in the model and normalized.

Most illustrations of canonical synthesis found in textbooks use simple examples with few or no complications. The following example is much closer to the real-world problems that may be encountered. It relates to the hotel case study described earlier. We will also modify the usual approach and normalize each user view separately before combining all the user views into a single schema.

An entity-relationship diagram can have only three types of entities: independent, dependent and relationship. A canonical data model is an elaboration of an E-R diagram which has been normalized. We will use these basic entity characteristics to develop our canonical data models using the following steps:

1. Identify all the independent entities named in the user view and set them up as parents.

2. Identify all the dependent entities named in the view and add them to the model showing the parent-child relationships.

3. Identify all the relationship entities named in the view and add them to the model and indicate the entity-to-entity relationships.

4. Examine each relationship entity and identify the data elements that make up its key or serve as foreign keys. Name the entities that are associated through this relationship entity. If any of these entities are not shown on the model, add them in as parents and indicate the relationships between the entities.

5. Expand all the entities in the data model to include their keys and data attributes.

6. Normalize each family independently.

7. Combine all the normalized user views into a single canonical data model as follows:

a. Put each independent entity on a separate page and enter its family, including the relationship entities.

b. Draw an ellipse around each relationship entity to highlight it.

c. Expand each entity once. When entities are repeated, cross-reference them to the first occurrence.

The canonical data model or subschema that models a particular user view must contain all data needed to produce the user view, even if the data are not shown in the user view. This means that the user view must be analyzed before it is modeled, and the model must be checked against the user view to ensure the user view can be produced from it.

The reader should note that the terms *entity* and *record* are both used in the discussion. The distinction is that entity is the real-world situation that is described by a record which has a key and possibly one or more data attributes.

For our example of canonical synthesis, we use five reports produced for hotel management at the head office and at the hotel franchise level.

Report #1—A monthly report on franchises and franchise fees. This report indicates the outstanding balance on franchise fees for each franchise hotel and includes the franchisee's name, and the total debits and credits. It is illustrated in Figure 5.6A.

<u>Monthly Report on Franchises and Franchise Fees</u>

Month/Year -------

Franchise	Franchisee Name	Hotel Name	Total Debits	Total Credits	Outstanding Balance
----	----	----	----	----	----
----	----	----	----	----	----
----	----	----	----	----	----

Figure 5.6A

Report #2—Monthly hotel inspections report. This report records the inspections done at the different hotels and provides a rating on a sliding scale. It is illustrated in Figure 5.7A.

<u>Monthly Hotel Inspections Report</u>

Month/Year ----   Hotel Name -----

Hotel Location ----   Average Inspection
                                                   Rating ------

Inspection Date	Inspected Area	Inspected Area Rating
----	----	----
----	----	----
----	----	----

Figure 5.7A

Report #3—Hotel monthly equipment rental. This report lists the type of equipment rented at each hotel with the hours and fees collected. It is illustrated in Figure 5.8A.

```
Hotel Monthly Equipment Rental

Month/Year  ----                            Hotel Name  ----

Equipment Type              Hours Rented              Fees
---------------------------------------------------------------
----                        ----                      ----
----                        ----                      ----
----                        ----                      ----
```

Figure 5.8A

Report #4—Hotel monthly customer profile. This report provides information on the hotel customers. It is illustrated in Figure 5.9A.

```
Hotel Monthly Customer Profile

Month/Year  ----                            Hotel Name  ----

Customer   Customer Type       Number    City From    Type of
Name       (Business,          of Days                Payment
           Conference,                                (Company
           Tourist,                                   Invoice,
           Personal)                                  Cash,
                                                       Credit
                                                       Card)
---------------------------------------------------------------------
----       ----                ----      ----         ----
----       ----                ----      ----         ----
----       ----                ----      ----         ----
```

Figure 5.9A

Report #5—Monthly hotel occupancy summary. This report compares the available rooms in a hotel with the actual occupancy. It is illustrated in Figure 5.10A.

```
Monthly Hotel Occupancy Summary

Month/Year  ----

Hotel Name      Location        Possible            Actual
                                Occupancy Days      Occupancy Days
---------------------------------------------------------------------
----            ----            ----                ----
----            ----            ----                ----
----            ----            ----                ----
```

Figure 5.10A

Report #1—Monthly report on franchises and franchise fees (Figure 5.6A). This report provides information on two independent entities: franchisee and hotel. It also provides information on franchise, which is a relationship entity. This franchise information includes the total debits and credits associated with franchise fees due, and the outstanding balance. The outstanding balance is updated from the total receivables and payments. So provision must be made in the model for receivables data.

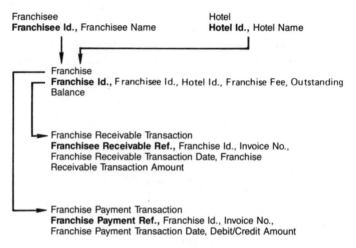

Franchisee
Franchisee Id., Franchisee Name

Hotel
Hotel Id., Hotel Name

Franchise
Franchise Id., Franchisee Id., Hotel Id., Franchise Fee, Outstanding Balance

Franchise Receivable Transaction
Franchisee Receivable Ref., Franchise Id., Invoice No., Franchise Receivable Transaction Date, Franchise Receivable Transaction Amount

Franchise Payment Transaction
Franchise Payment Ref., Franchise Id., Invoice No., Franchise Payment Transaction Date, Debit/Credit Amount

Figure 5.6B

The normalized data model is illustrated in Figure 5.6B. The two independent entities, franchisee and hotel, are shown with the only data known about them from the report, that is, the franchisee name and the hotel name. To identify these entities easily, we have added keys, "Franchisee Id." and "Hotel Id."

Franchise is shown as a relationship entity joining franchisee and hotel. We include "Franchise Id." as the key, and "Franchisee Id." and "Hotel Id." as foreign keys to point to the entities related. "Franchise Fee" and "Outstanding Balance" are the only attributes known from the report.

We also include two other records: The first is franchise receivable transaction with receivables information. These data include the date the receivable was due, the amount and the invoice number. The record is identified by the "Franchise Receivable Ref." and "Franchise Id." is a foreign key which indicates that this record is a child of franchise. "Franchise Id." is not part of the key because "Franchise Receivable Ref." is sufficient to identify the record.

The second record is franchise payment transaction which provides payment information. This includes the date payment was made, the amount debited or credited and the invoice number. "Franchise Id." is a foreign key which indicates that this record is a child of franchise.

"Invoice No.," found in both franchise receivable transaction and franchise payable transaction, is a foreign key pointing to "Invoice." "Invoice" is included because receivables and payments stem from invoices. However, unlike "Franchise Id." which is mandatory when franchise receivable transaction is created, "Invoice No." is optional and is added only when the invoice is prepared later.

Report #2—Monthly hotel inspections report (Figure 5.7A).   This report provides information on one independent entity: hotel. A hotel can be inspected many times and each inspection can include several areas in the hotel.

Hotel
Hotel Id., Hotel Name, Location

Hotel Inspection
Hotel Inspection Ref., Hotel Id., Hotel Inspection Date

Inspected Area Status
Hotel Inspection Ref., Area Id., Inspection Rating

Figure 5.7B

The normalized data model is illustrated in Figure 5.7B. The data model is a simple tree structure with "Hotel" as the parent and "Hotel Inspection" as its child. "Hotel Inspection," in turn, has "Inspected Area Status" as its child.

From the report, the hotel attributes are hotel name and location. "Hotel Inspection" is identified by "Hotel Inspection Ref." "Hotel Inspection Date" is the only attribute found in the report. "Hotel Id." is shown as a foreign key to show that "Hotel Inspection" is a child of "Hotel." "Inspected Area Status" is identified by "Hotel Inspection Ref." and "Area Id. Inspection Rating" is the only attribute.

Report #3—Hotel monthly equipment rental (Figure 5.8A).   On the surface, this report would appear to have two independent entities: hotel and hotel equipment type. Discussing this report with the user, we found that equipment type is charged differently by each hotel. This dependency is reflected by hotel equipment type becoming a child of hotel.

The report provides the hours rented and the fees charged for the rental. For this we need rental information. Rental can occur only if a cus-

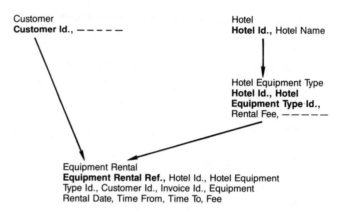

Figure 5.8B

tomer is involved. So, now we have two independent entities: hotel and customer.

The normalized data model is shown in Figure 5.8B. No specific information is included about customers in the report, so customer is described only by the "Customer Id." key. Hotel is described by "Hotel Name."

Hotel equipment type is identified by "Hotel Id." and "Hotel Equipment Type Id." Its only attribute is "Rental Fee."

Equipment rental is a relationship entity linking customer and hotel equipment type. Its attributes are "Equipment Rental Date," "Time From," "Time To" and "Fee." Foreign keys included are "Hotel Id." and "Hotel Equipment Id." to point to hotel equipment type, and "Customer Id." to point to customer. "Invoice No." is a foreign key pointing to invoice. Invoice is included because rental is charged to the customer.

Report #4—Hotel monthly customer profile (Figure 5.9A). This report provides information on two independent entities: hotel and customer. City is not an independent entity because our interest in it is restricted to the customer's place of residence.

This report provides information on the number of days a customer stayed in the hotel, so occupancy data are required. It also provides information on the type of payment made.

Figure 5.9B illustrates the normalized data model. Customer is identified by "Customer Id." and is described by "Customer Name," "Customer Type" and "City." Hotel is identified by "Hotel Id." and described by "Hotel Name."

Hotel room is a child of hotel and is identified by "Hotel Id." and "Room Id." No attributes are included in the report.

Room occupancy is a relationship entity between hotel and customer. It is identified by "Room Occupancy Ref." Its attributes are "Room Occu-

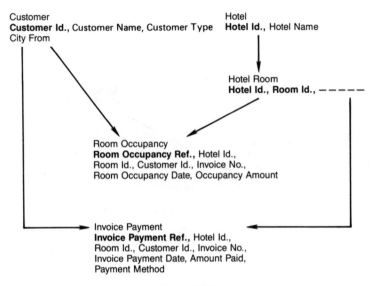

Figure 5.9B

pancy Date" and "Occupancy Amount." "Hotel Id." and "Room Id." are foreign keys pointing to hotel room. "Customer Id." is a foreign key pointing to customer. "Invoice No." is a foreign key providing a cross-reference to invoice. It is included as room occupancy is charged to the customer.

Invoice payment is a relationship entity between hotel and customer. Its attributes are "Invoice Payment Date," "Amount Paid" and "Payment Method." "Hotel Id." and "Room Id." are foreign keys pointing to hotel room. "Customer Id." is a foreign key pointing to customer. "Invoice No." is a foreign key providing a cross-reference to customer invoice.

Report #5—Monthly hotel occupancy summary (Figure 5.10A).   This report is similar to Report #4 as occupancy data are required which indicate the need to include the customer entity in the data model.

The normalized data model is shown in Figure 5.10B. Customer, hotel, hotel room and room occupancy have the same structure as Report #4, except no payment data are shown as fewer data attributes are known from the report.

"Invoice No." is included as a foreign key in several of the relationship entities in the example for the sake of data completeness. However, the invoice entity is not shown in the data model because it is not needed specifically to produce the reports.

To consolidate the subschemas from Reports #1–5, we take each primary entity and create a separate family consolidating all the dependent and relationship entities with their attributes. Each relationship entity entered is highlighted. Any records occurring in more than one family are expanded

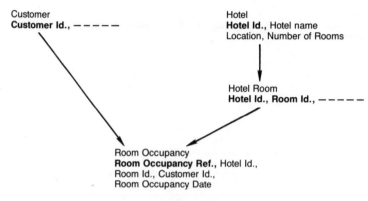

Figure 5.10B

only once so that the data are not duplicated under each primary entity. Figure 5.11 Parts 1–6 illustrate this consolidation. This approach to drawing the canonical model emphasizing independent (primary), dependent and relationship entities results in well-organized and easy-to-understand data models.

When canonical synthesis is done manually, it can be both time consuming and frustrating if one is consolidating a large number of possible user views or subschemas. Software is available which has been specifically designed to make this task easier. One such product is called Data Designer (6) from Knowledgeware Inc. An effective data dictionary or even an unsophisticated sort program could reduce copying, sorting and the manual errors to make this task easier.

Figure 5.11 Part 1

Hotel
(See Part 1)

Hotel Inspection
Hotel Inspection Ref., Hotel Id., Hotel Inspection Date

Inspected Area Status
Hotel Inspection Ref., Area Id., Inspection Rating

Figure 5.11 Part 2

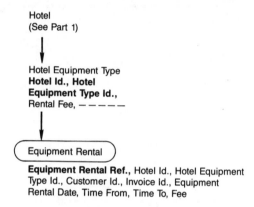

Hotel
(See Part 1)

Hotel Equipment Type
**Hotel Id., Hotel
Equipment Type Id.**,
Rental Fee, – – – – –

Equipment Rental

Equipment Rental Ref., Hotel Id., Hotel Equipment
Type Id., Customer Id., Invoice Id., Equipment
Rental Date, Time From, Time To, Fee

Figure 5.11 Part 3

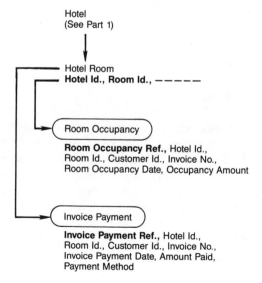

Hotel
(See Part 1)

Hotel Room
Hotel Id., Room Id., – – – – –

Room Occupancy

Room Occupancy Ref., Hotel Id.,
Room Id., Customer Id., Invoice No.,
Room Occupancy Date, Occupancy Amount

Invoice Payment

Invoice Payment Ref., Hotel Id.,
Room Id., Customer Id., Invoice No.,
Invoice Payment Date, Amount Paid,
Payment Method

Figure 5.11 Part 4

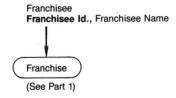

Figure 5.11 Part 5

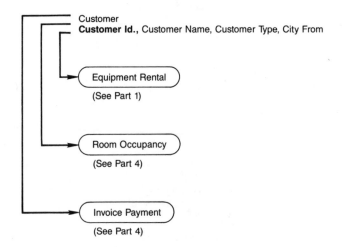

Figure 5.11 Part 6

5.6 REFERENTIAL INTEGRITY

Relational data base management systems have brought with them many advantages. They also have certain disadvantages, one of which is the problem caused by lack of referential integrity. This occurs when it is possible to create or retain records in file which owe their existence to other records which are not in file. This places a burden on the data administrator to manually control these dependent and relationship records when this function should be performed by the data base management system. The concept of referential integrity is best illustrated by example. Consider the following set of records:

Hotel
  Hotel Id., Hotel Name, Hotel Location

Hotel Room
  Hotel Id., Room Id., -------

In a hierarchical or network data base, hotel room could not be put into the data base unless hotel was already there because hotel room is dependent on hotel. Similarly, if the hotel record were deleted, hotel room would automatically be deleted. This control does not exist in a relational data base, and hotel room could both be established and not be deleted if the hotel record does not exist. This situation is called a lack of referential integrity and it has proven to be a major problem to be overcome by the relational data base management system designers.

The preceding example is relatively simple. The problem becomes more complex when foreign keys are involved. Consider the following examples:

---

1 Hotel
      Hotel Id., Hotel Name, Hotel Location

   Hotel Inspection
      Hotel Inspection Ref., Date, Hotel Id.

2 Franchise
      Franchise Id., Franchisee Id., Hotel Id., Franchise Fee

3 Franchise Receivable Transaction
      Franchise Payment Ref., Franchise Id., Date,   Debit/Credit
      Amount, Invoice No.

In the first example, "Hotel Id." is a foreign key in "Hotel Inspection." Strictly speaking, it should be part of the key. It is not because "Hotel Inspection Ref." can be made unique and it is simpler to use a key that is a single data element. In a hierarchical or network data base, "Hotel Inspection" would be a child of hotel and the need for "Hotel Id." as a foreign key would be eliminated. In a relational data base, the problem of referential integrity arises, as there is no control over the creation or deletion of "Hotel Inspection" tied to hotel. Also, in this situation, "Hotel Id." is mandatory when "Hotel Inspection" is entered to indicate where the inspection was done.

The second example illustrates a relationship entity, franchise, which is identified by a unique reference, "Franchise Id." The foreign keys "Franchisee Id." and "Hotel Id." would logically have made up the key and, hence, must have values assigned when the record is created. These foreign keys would be eliminated in a hierarchical or network data base but create the problem of referential integrity in a relational data base if they are omitted, or if either the hotel or franchisee records are deleted.

In the third example, "Franchise Id." is a foreign key which is mandatory because it would logically be part of the key to the record. "Invoice No.," on the other hand, serves only as cross-reference to invoice when an invoice is prepared. Should an invoice not be prepared, it will never be established. Hence, it is a foreign key which is optional, that is, its absence does not create the problem of referential integrity.

REFERENCES

1. ANSI/X3/SPARC (American National Standards Institute/Standards Planning and Requirements Committee) DBMS Framework, "Report of the Study Group on Database Management Systems," ed. Dennis Tsichritzis and Anthony Klug, University of Toronto, Toronto, Canada. AFIPS PRESS, 210 Summit Avenue, Montvale, NJ 07645, 1978.

2. James Martin, *Managing the Data-Base Environment,* (Englewood Cliffs, NJ: Prentice-Hall, Inc., 1983).

3. James Martin, *Computer Data-Base Organization,* 2nd ed., (Englewood Cliffs, NJ: Prentice-Hall, Inc., 1975).

4. Peter P. Chen, "A Preliminary Framework for Entity-Relationship Models," in *Entity-Relationship Approach to Information Modeling and Analysis,* ed. P. P. Chen (Amsterdam, North-Holland, 1983).

5. E. F. Codd, "Further Normalization of the Data Base Relational Model," in *Courant Computer Science Symposia,* Vol. 6: "Data Base Systems," ed. R. Rustin, (Englewood Cliffs, NJ: Prentice-Hall, Inc., 1972). Adapted by permission of Prentice-Hall, Inc.

6. Information on DATA DESIGNER available from Knowledgeware Inc., 2020 Hogback Road, Ann Arbor, MI 48104.

6
The Information Resource Management Process: Strategic Planning

SP2   The Information Architecture

In this chapter, we examine the information resource management activities at the strategic planning level. Table 6.1 highlights the IRM outputs produced at this level.

Before we examine the IRM activities, let us recall our understanding of information resource management from Chapter 5. In the information architecture (Figure 4.2), the business organization and where it is going is reflected in its mission and objectives. Analyzing the business, we identify the high-level or corporate functions it performs. These functions in turn provide us with business applications. The functions also provide us with the real-world entities that the business is concerned with. Modeling these entities, we get entity-relationship diagrams which are subdivided into logical sets of data called subject data bases. Business applications either update or use these subject data bases.

The functions associated with the business applications are expanded. This expansion identifies entities in the subject data bases as records with keys and data attributes. These subject data bases in turn are normalized to provide data models in their simplest form. These data models are then

TABLE 6.1 The STRIPE Matrix Highlighting the Information Resource Management Outputs During Strategic Planning

	Business	Data	Application	Technical Environment	Type of Plan
STRATEGIC PLANNING	SP1 Business Strategy: Mission Objectives and Goals Strategic Directions Critical Success Factors (CSFs) Major Information Requirements	SP2 Data Architecture: Primary Entities Crown E-R Diagram Subject Data Bases	SP2 Application Architecture: Business Applications	SP3 Technical Architecture: Function Distribution Computers and Peripherals Data Distribution Communications Software (DBMS, Dictionary, Security) Office Automation	SP4 Migration Plan: Major Projects over a 3–5 year period
	SP2 Major Functions (Processes) SP4 User and MIS Department Evaluation SP4 Proposed Organizations		SP4 Current Application Evaluation	SP4 Evaluation of Current Hardware/Software, Communications and Office Automation	
TACTICAL PLANNING	TP1 Function Expansion TP1 ASDM Policy TP1 Organization Change: IRM Function Education Function Strategic Planning Function Quality Assurance	TP2 Logical Data Bases: Entity Expansion Current Files/ Documents Comparison Data Normalization Data Distribution	TP3 Physical Application Definition	TP4 Hardware/Software Communications/ Office Automation Specifications TP5 Selection of: Computers, etc. Communications Equipment Software Office Automation Equipment and Software	SP5 Budget Year Plan: (or similar period) Prioritized Projects scheduled and resourced
OPERATIONAL PLANNING	OP2 Business System Specifications: Activity Level Functions Output Requirements Output Design OP9 System Implementation: Manual Procedures D.P. Operations Procedures Education OP7 System Test: Testing OP10 System Review: Business Needs Operating Efficiency	OP4 Physical Data Base Design: Activity Level Data Expansion Data Volumes Data Accesses Physical Data Bases Physical DB Access Modules OP7 Testing OP9 File Conversion	OP3 Procedure Design: Event and External Action/Condition Analysis Embryonic Procedures Menu Hierarchies Input Screens and Forms OP5 Procedure Expansion: File Update Logic Output Logic OP6 System Construction: Physical Procedures OP8 Package Acquisition OP7 System Test: Testing OP9 Production Libraries	OP11 Product Implementation: Product Acquisition Product Installation Product Conversion Product Testing	OP1 Individual Project Plans

analyzed in terms of the real-world actions and conditions which trigger data creation or change. This analysis results in the definition of basic or embryonic procedures within the business applications.

This completes the information resource management process. In application development, these logical data models and business applications are converted into physical application systems which run on computers and provide information to manage and operate the business.

In information resource management, we are concerned with function and data at the conceptual or logical level. In this context, see Table 6.1, the STRIPE matrix, the information resource management outputs at the strategic planning level are the major functions, the data architecture and the application architecture. All these are obtained during Phase SP2.

If an organization does not wish to develop a strategic information resource plan (SIRP) but still wishes to implement information resource management, Phase SP2 must still be completed. The only situation when it may be omitted would be if conventional application system design is done where the data are derived as a byproduct of the system processes. The cost of this approach will be reflected in data inconsistency, incompatibility and redundancy.

We will use the hotel case study described in Chapter 5 to illustrate the activities in these phases.

6.1 STRATEGIC PLANNING

SP2.1 Identify the Organization's Functions

The first step is to identify the highest-level functions the business carries out. These functions may not reflect the people organization. The primary functions performed by the hotel chain at the corporate and hotel levels are:

CORPORATE LEVEL

Financial Services
Marketing
Hotel Construction
Franchise Sales
Franchise Management
Room Reservations and Occupancy
Head Office Administration

HOTEL LEVEL

Financial Services
Room Reservations and Occupancy

Equipment Management

Recreation

Shop Management

Restaurant Management

External Services

Hotel Administration

These functions can be expanded into a series of hierarchies. Table 6.2 is an extract from a function hierarchy. This function expansion should be done to about the middle management level. In a very large organization, it may be restricted to senior management levels.

SP2.2 Identify the Entities from the Functions

The real-world entities about which information is needed to perform these functions are identified. The term *entity* is used in a very general sense at this level and distinctions between such items as entities, relationship entities, forms, screens, and so on may be ignored. It is sufficient to name all the "things" that come to mind in terms of each function. This exercise is very much a fishing expedition and we will sort through and clean up the "entities" in the next procedure.

Each function level links to one or more entities (Table 6.3). It is very likely that entities will be replicated during this exercise.

SP2.3 Identify the Primary Entities and Form the Crown

The list of entities are reviewed and the key entities such as customer, supplier, and product are identified and associated to form the "crown" or apex of the entity family.

TABLE 6.2   Natural Function Hierarchy

Financial Services
  Accounts Receivable
  Accounts Payable
  General Ledger
  Investments
  Payroll
  Cash Management
  Budget
    Annual Budget Preparation
    Annual Budget Approval
    Annual Budget Implementation
      Monthly Budget Calendarization
      Monthly Budget Compared with Monthly Expenses
      Corrective Action

TABLE 6.3 Capturing Functions and Entities

Functions	Entities
1 *Corporate Level*	
Financial Services	
Budget	Income
Accounts Receivable	Expenses
Accounts Payable	Profit
General Ledger	Assets
Investments	Tax
Payroll	Chart of Accounts Item
Cash Management	Cost Center
Marketing	
Sales	Location
Advertising	Hotel
Media	Accommodation
Information Brochure	Bedroom
	Meeting/Banquet Room
	Customer
	Vendor
	Restaurant
	Food
	Shop

(Note: Functions and entities are listed as they are identified.
Items on the same line do not imply separate dependencies. It
should be emphasized that these are preliminary lists and can
and will be added to as the design process continues.)

This crown should reflect the essence of the business. It serves two
purposes: (1) to provide executive management with a high-level view of the
business and (2) to provide the basis for building a complete E-R model
reflecting the business in terms of its entities and their relationships.

The crown for the hotel example is illustrated in Figure 6.1. Since the
data model is at the highest possible level, the entity associations may be
shown with simple lines joining the entities in a network.

SP2.4 Develop Function Hierarchies and Entity Families

The function hierarchies from SP2.1 are refined. Entities from SP2.2 are
reviewed and duplicated entities are eliminated. The entities are reorganized
into natural families. Within these families, entities will occur in common.
These entities are possible relationship entities linking two or more different
entities together. Each entity family is now drawn as a separate data model.

This modeling is done following the same principles defined in Section
5.3 (Entity-Relationship Diagrams) using the STRIPE technique where we
stated that an entity must be independent, dependent or a relationship. This

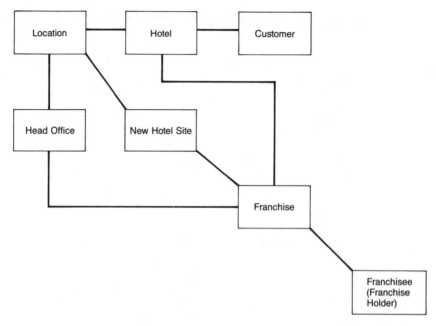

Figure 6.1   Vacation hotels—primary entities related

principle is applied to the entities listed. First, the independent entities are identified. These are put at the top of a column or page. Next, the dependent entities are identified and the entity families are built. Dependent entities which occur in more than one family are candidates for relationship entities.

Table 6.4 illustrates the hotel entity families. Table 6.5 is an example of a financial entity family. The common entities are shown in bold print. The financial family is very important as many nonfinancial entities are linked to financial entities. Unfortunately, this is often ignored as it is assumed that accounting systems are all alike and can be acquired or developed without linking financial data to the organization's entity-relationship diagram (corporate data model).

The entity families are drawn as separate data models within the E-R diagram. Figures 6.2 and 6.3 illustrate the hotel and the hotel financial entities. In most situations, information will be required on all the entities identified. Occasionally, it may not be required for certain primary or dependent entities. For example, no data may be needed about the enterprise or corporation itself. When such situations occur, these entities should still be identified and modeled but should also be marked with an asterisk so that the model will be complete at all times.

TABLE 6.4   Vacation
Hotels—Entity
Hierarchy

Location
  Head Office
    Staff Services
      Salaries
      Benefits
      Pensions
      Education
      Work schedules
    New Hotel Site
      Plans
      Blueprints
      Building permits
      Construction
    Hotel
      Staff Services
        Salaries
        Benefits
        Pensions
        Education
        Work schedules
      Franchise
        Franchise fees
      Hotel Inspections
      Equipment
  Franchise Holder
    Franchise
      Franchise fee
  Staff
    Salaries
    Benefits
    Pensions
    Education
    Work schedules

SP2.5 Highlight the Common Entities and Complete the E-R Diagram

The common entities within the data model families are highlighted to indicate the possible relationships between the data models. This highlighting is shown by drawing ellipses around the possible relationship entities in the data models in Figures 6.2 and 6.3. The result is the completed E-R diagram. This diagram will probably change as more information becomes known about the business.

TABLE 6.5   Financial
Entities

Department (Cost Center)
Investments
Assets
Profit/Loss
Transaction Type
  Budgeted Income
  Actual Income
    Charge
  Other Income
    Franchise fees
    Rent
  Budgeted Expenses
  Actual Expenses
    Salaries
    Taxes
    Benefits
    Pensions
    Purchases
Chart of Accounts
  Charge
  Franchise fees
  Rent
  Salaries
  Taxes
  Benefits
  Pensions
  Purchases

SP2.6 Divide the E-R Diagram into Subject Data Bases

The E-R diagram is too large to analyze and expand all at once. The entities can be grouped into sets which relate to particular subjects. These subjects, in turn, relate to business functions which can also be grouped into sets called business applications. These business applications can be defined so that specific applications primarily update specific subject data bases. The grouping of subject data bases and business applications is an iterative process.

To start off, group entities into subsets within the data families to obtain the first series of subject data bases. Subject data bases should include parent-child sets only, that is, they should not jump from one family tree to another. They can also contain relationship entities which would be repeated in different entity families.

Subject data bases can be identified on the E-R diagram by circling the concerned entity sets. Circling makes for messy diagramming and may not

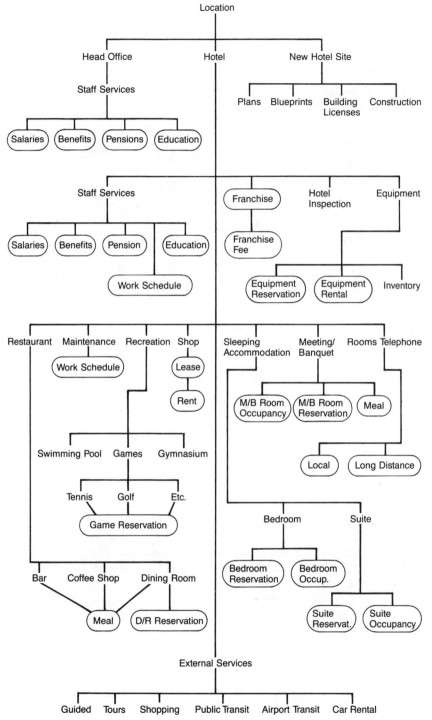

Figure 6.2 Vacation Hotels Corporate Entity-Relationship Model

NOTE: 'Charges' for service not shown but assumed.

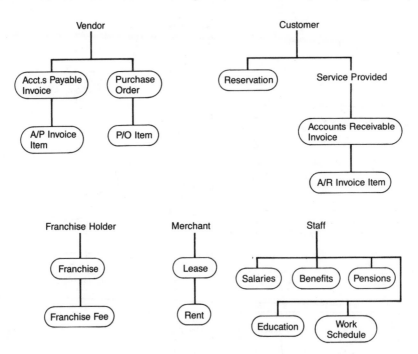

Figure 6.2 (*Continued*)

be needed if each subject data base is a complete arm of a family and is identified by the parent entity in that arm. Table 6.6 lists the subject data bases for the Vacation Hotels.

SP2.7 Identify Business Applications

An organization usually has many application systems already functioning which meet some of its information needs. However, for planning purposes, it is worthwhile putting these aside and identifying a new set of application systems to meet those needs. Later, in the migration strategy, a decision could be made to retain unchanged or to modify existing applications, or to develop completely new applications.

In order to obtain the best grouping of applications or associated function sets, they are identified by the users with the help of the:

1. Objectives and critical success factors defined in the business strategy.

2. Functions performed.

3. The corporate entity-relationship diagram.

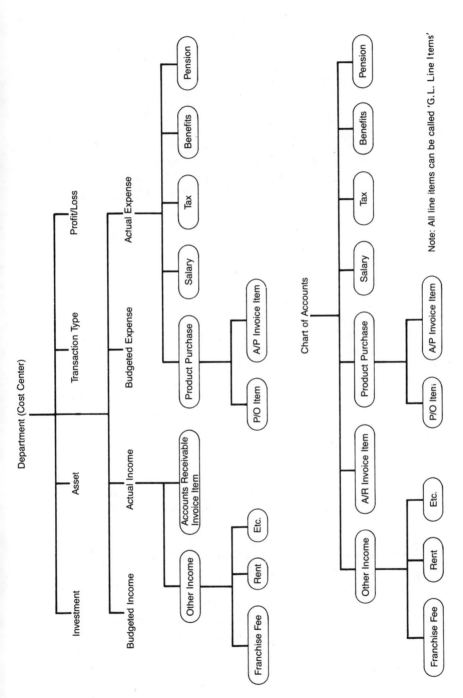

Figure 6.3 Financial entities

77

TABLE 6.6 Subject Data Bases

---

 1 Location
 2 Hotel Construction
 3 Franchise Data
 4 Staff Data
 5 Equipment Data
 6 Recreation
 7 Shop
 8 Sleeping Accommodation
 9 Meeting/Banquet Room
10 Restaurant
11 External Services
12 Customer
13 Vendor
14 Financial
15 Tax Table
16 Maintenance (Work Schedule)
17 Telephone Service

Table 6.7 illustrates how this is done. We examine each of the business objectives and critical success factors in turn to determine which applications come to mind. We then independently review the function hierarchies and record a new group of applications. Finally, we repeat the exercise for the corporate entity-relationship diagram. As we saw when identifying entities earlier, the same applications may be detected from more than one source.

SP2.8 Review and Refine the List of Applications

The list of applications is refined to eliminate duplicates. The remaining applications are named. These applications are described briefly and their scope is defined. Table 6.8 illustrates the refined application grouping for the hotel.

SP2.9 Group Applications under Major Organizational
Functions and by Location

Since priorities must be set later for new application development and major modification of existing applications, the applications must be categorized. The first step is to organize them into groups under major organizational functions as illustrated in the hotel example (Table 6.8). In this example, we have also indicated whether the applications apply to the head office, the hotel or to both. The latter information will be useful in the analysis of distributed data needs.

TABLE 6.7   Identifying Business Applications

Sources: 1   Objectives and Critical Success Factors (CSFs)
            2   Functions
            3   Corporate Entity-Relationship Diagram

1   *Objectives and CSFs*

Marketing
Hotel Construction
Quality Control
Productivity Measurement

2   *Functions*

Financial
   Budget
   Payroll
   Accounts Receivable
   Accounts Payable
   General Ledger
   Investments
   Cash Management
   Purchasing
   Staff Pensions
Marketing
   Sales
   Advertising

3   *Corporate Entity-Relationship Diagram*

Financial
   Budget
   Accounts Payable
   Accounts Receivable
   Purchasing
   Investments
   Payroll
   Pensions
   Tax Table
Franchise Management
Personnel
Hotel Construction
Sleeping Accommodation Reservations and Occupancy
Meeting/Banquet Room Reservations and Occupancy

SP2.10 Group Applications under System Type
(management, information, office and process control)

A further analysis of the sets of applications indicates whether they are management, information or office systems (Table 6.9). A fourth category may also be included, that of process control systems, if the organization

TABLE 6.8 Consolidated and Refined Business
Applications (Head Office and Hotel)

Application	Head off.	Hotel
01 Financial		
01 Budget	*	*
02 Payroll	*	*
03 Accounts Receivable	*	*
04 Accounts Payable	*	*
05 General Ledger	*	*
06 Investments	*	*
07 Cash Management	*	*
08 Purchasing	*	*
09 Staff Pensions	*	*
10 Tax Table	*	*
02 Marketing		
01 Sales	*	
02 Advertising	*	
03 Hotel Construction		
01 Hotel Construction	*	

TABLE 6.9 Consolidated and Refined Business Applications
(Management, Information and Office Systems)

Application	Management Systems	Information Systems	Office Systems
01 Financial			
01 Budget	*		*
02 Payroll		*	
03 Accounts Receivable		*	
04 Accounts Payable		*	
05 General Ledger		*	
06 Investments		*	*
07 Cash Management		*	
08 Purchasing		*	
09 Staff Pensions		*	
10 Tax Table		*	
02 Marketing			
01 Sales		*	
02 Advertising		*	
03 Hotel Construction			
01 Hotel Construction		*	

uses them. Grouping these applications into these categories aids in the decision to be made later to allocate priorities for development.

Management systems include applications that help the management process such as planning, budgeting, and control and performance reporting. Information systems provide information to support the business processes, such as production, reservations, and accounts receivable. Office systems use information technology to improve organizational performance by providing computer access to all levels of management and workers on microcomputers, for example, electronic spreadsheet, word processing, electronic mail, electronic calendar and decision support. Process control systems result in automatically changing an ongoing operation rather than producing human readable output. They generally use complex logic and need minimal data storage, such as radar navigation, traffic control, and elevator systems.

Some systems may fall into more than one category but this is not critical. The purpose of categorization is to set priorities for later development.

SP2.11 Link Applications to Subject Data Bases

Up to this point in time, we have defined entities and subject data bases which group entities into logical sets. We have also defined applications and have grouped them by major organizational function. An image appears of an immense data structure and large numbers of applications that need to be built to interact with this data structure to service the organization's management, information and office systems' needs.

It is neither practical nor possible to put all the organization's data into one physical data base. How does one build a series of physical data bases without data inconsistency, redundancy and incompatabilty? When should these physical data bases be built?

The answer to the first question is to put all the data defined in the subject data bases into a data dictionary and have their use controlled by a data administrator. The answer to the second is to link the subject data bases to the individual applications in terms of predominant data creation or data use. The "create" applications add, delete or modify records in the data bases. The "use" applications access the data but do not change them. This is illustrated in Table 6.10. (Table 6.11 shows this table inverted). The applications now dictate which subject data bases should be built and in what sequence. A particular subject data base may become a single physical data base, be split into more than one, or two or more subject data bases may be combined.

It is good practice to have only one application perform most of the updates in a particular subject data base. Sequencing this information by subject data base provides a table (Table 6.11) which indicates the applica-

TABLE 6.10 Consolidated and Refined Business Applications Linked with Subject Data Bases

	Application	Subject create	Data base use
01	Financial		
	01 Budget	14	14
	02 Payroll	14	15,4
	03 Accounts Receivable	14	12
	04 Accounts Payable	14	13
	05 General Ledger	14	14
	06 Investments	14	14
	07 Cash Management	14	14
	08 Purchasing	14	14,13
	09 Staff Pensions	14	14,4
	10 Tax Table	15	*
02	Marketing		
	01 Sales	1,2,5,6,7, 8,9,10,11,12	
	02 Advertising	-do-	
03	Hotel Construction		
	01 Hotel Construction	2	

tion or applications that update a particular subject data base. If more than one application updates a subject data base, it is worthwhile examining the applications again to see whether they should be combined.

With the completion of this step, we have obtained the primary outputs of the information architecture phase:

TABLE 6.11 Subject Data Bases with Related Applications

	Subject data base	Application create	Use
1	Location	03.01	02.01,02.02 05.01
2	Hotel Construction	03.01	02.01,02.02
3	Franchise Data	04.01–04.04, 05.01	05.01
4	Staff Data	14.01	01.02,01.09 14.02
5	Equipment Data	07.01,07.02	02.01,02.02
6	Recreation	08.01	02.01,02.02
7	Shop	09.01	02.01,02.02
8	Sleeping Accommodation	06.01	02.01,02.02 04.01–04.04
9	Meeting/Banquet Room	06.02	02.01,02.02

- to define the application systems,
- to define the subject data bases, and
- to associate the application systems with the subject data bases.

The next stage in the development of the information architecture is the expansion of the entities in each subject data base into records with keys and data attributes, and then to normalize the data and obtain canonical data structures. This is covered in Chapter 7 as part of the tactical planning process.

7
The Information Resource Management Process: Tactical Planning

TP1 Function Expansion
TP2 Logical Data Base Design
TP3 Physical Application Definition

The tactical planning level of STRIPE includes those activities which link the organization's MIS strategic plans with actual system development and implementation. From the information resource management perspective, this includes the expansion of business functions, the design and development of all logical data bases, and the definition of the physical applications. Table 7.1 indicates the IRM outputs produced during tactical planning.

Phases TP1 (Function Expansion) and TP2 (Logical Data Base Design) are essential components of information resource management. Function expansion provides an understanding of the business reflected in the expansion of the entities in the subject data bases into normalized records which are described with keys and attributes. This is a top-down approach to logical data base design.

An alternative method of developing the logical data bases is to use canonical synthesis described in Chapter 5. The weakness of the latter is that

	Business	Data	Application	Technical Environment	Type of Plan
STRATEGIC PLANNING	SP1 Business Strategy: Mission Objectives and Goals Strategic Directions Critical Success Factors (CSFs) Major Information Requirements SP2 Major Functions (Processes) SP4 User and MIS Department Evaluation SP4 Proposed Organizations	SP2 Data Architecture: Primary Entities Crown E-R Diagram Subject Data Bases	SP2 Application Architecture: Business Applications SP4 Current Application Evaluation	SP3 Technical Architecture: Function Distribution Computers and Peripherals Data Distribution Communications Software (DBMS, Dictionary, Security) Office Automation SP4 Evaluation of Current Hardware/Software, Communications and Office Automation	SP4 Migration Plan: Major Projects over a 3–5 year period
TACTICAL PLANNING	TP1 Function Expansion TP1 ASDM Policy TP1 Organization Change: IRM Function Education Function Strategic Planning Function Quality Assurance	TP2 Logical Data Bases: Entity Expansion Current Files/Documents Comparison Data Normalization Data Distribution	TP3 Physical Application Definition	TP4 Hardware/Software Communications/Office Automation Specifications TP5 Selection of: Computers, etc. Communications Equipment Software Office Automation Equipment and Software	SP5 Budget Year Plan: (or similar period) Prioritized Projects scheduled and resourced OP1 Individual Project Plans
OPERATIONAL PLANNING	OP2 Business System Specifications: Activity Level Functions Output Requirements Output Design OP9 System Implementation: Manual Procedures D.P. Operations Procedures Education OP7 System Test: Testing OP10 System Review: Business Needs Operating Efficiency	OP4 Physical Data Base Design: Activity Level Data Expansion Data Volumes Data Accesses Physical Data Bases Physical DB Access Modules OP7 Testing OP9 File Conversion	OP3 Procedure Design: Event and External Action/Condition Analysis Embryonic Procedures Menu Hierarchies Input Screens and Forms OP5 Procedure Expansion: File Update Logic Output Logic OP6 System Construction: Physical Procedures OP8 Package Acquisition OP7 System Test: Testing OP9 Production Libraries	OP11 Product Implementation: Product Acquisition Product Installation Product Conversion Product Testing	

it is derived from "user views" which are specific to application systems. Therefore, it does not provide a corporate or enterprise perspective, even though this is done under the umbrella of the corporate entity-relationship diagram developed at the strategic planning level.

Phase TP3 Physical Application Definition is part of the system design process as it describes the scope and the components of the proposed application systems. This phase can be equated to the system specification phase of a conventional application systems development methodology. See Table 12.2 which lists phases for a generic systems methodology and their corresponding outputs.

7.1 TACTICAL PLANNING

TP1.1 Expand Function Hierarchies

The function hierarchies defined during strategic planning are expanded to the levels of data update and data extraction. Different levels of functions result ranging from divisions through functional areas, processes, logical functions and activities of the organization. The detailed expansion of activities should occur only during actual application design as described at the operational level (OP2.1) of STRIPE.

The following example illustrates the different function levels:

```
Division—Marketing
Functional Area—Sales
Process—Sales Administration
Logical Function—Area Distribution
                —Salesman Control
                —Market Analysis
(Logical functions can cover several levels in the function hierarchy).
Activities—Maintain Record of Sales
          —Analyze Sales
```

To further assist in this function analysis, every entity within the business can be associated with four general processes: planning, acquisition, stewardship and disposal. Examples of such processes are:

Planning—Forecasting, Budgeting
Acquisition—Purchasing, Production, Hiring, Contracting
Stewardship—Maintenance, Warehousing, Investment, Marketing, Transportation
Disposal—Sales, Writeoff, Layoff, Destruction

Note: The next two activities, TP1.2 and TP1.3, are not part of function expansion, but are included in this phase as this is the first phase to be implemented in the tactical plans.

TP1.2 Establish a New MIS (Management Information Services) Organization

During SP4, the MIS organization was reviewed and improvements may have been recommended. These organizational changes should be put in place at this time.

TP1.3 Develop a Policy on Application System Development

The organization should develop a policy on application system development regarding the use of the development methodology as a set of guidelines or as standards. It should define the discretion to be vested in the project managers to adhere to the standards and to use design techniques best suited to solving the particular problem.

TP2.1 Expand the Subject Data Bases to Complete the Conceptual or Logical Data Base Structure

The corporate entity-relationship diagram was divided into subject data bases in SP2. These subject data bases are expanded to records with keys and attributes to complete the conceptual or logical data base structure.

Each function that has been defined is analyzed and new entities are defined. Within each subject data base, each entity is described in terms of its identifier or key and its attributes, creating a logical record. These entities will usually be further expanded during application system design.

In SP2, we indicated that information may not be required about certain entities such as the enterprise or organization, but that they should still be captured in the model for completeness. These entities would be marked by an asterisk in the model. If no record is to be maintained, these entities do not need to be described in terms of their keys and attributes.

The extent of the data expansion of the entities in a subject data base is directly dependent on the level of function analysis carried out. In the information architecture (SP2), the functions should have been defined only to a level where the organization's business is understandable. These functions should have resulted in corresponding entities being identified. During tactical planning (TP1.1), detailed function expansion occurs. These lower-level functions lead to detailed data requirements which could be either at the entity or data attribute level.

As function and entity expansion occurs, incremental levels of record definition may be used to develop system prototypes using only the data defined to that stage of entity expansion. This subject is covered in Chapter 12, "Prototyping Application Systems Development."

Each subject data base in the E-R diagram should have one or more hierarchical or linear sets of entities identified. For example, in the Vacation Hotels case study, let us consider the following subject data bases:

LOCATION

Location
   Head Office
   Hotel
   New Hotel Site

FRANCHISE DATA

Hotel
Franchise Holder (franchisee)
   Franchise
      Franchise Fee

SLEEPING ACCOMMODATION

Sleeping Accommodation
   Reservation
   Occupancy
      Charge

"Location" was identified as a subject data base. Whether it becomes a logical or physical data base would depend on the amount of information to be recorded about it. If all that is required is to know where the head office, hotel and new hotel site are situated, "Location" would become only an attribute of each of these three records and cease to be a subject data base.

Earlier, we stated that subject data bases should not usually embrace more than one family tree. "Franchise Data" includes two independent entities: "Hotel" and "Franchise Holder (franchisee)." This was done because the emphasis is on "Franchise" which associates the two entities. A decision should be made whether to retain "Franchise Data" as the subject data base with "Hotel" and "Franchise Holder" included or to remove "Hotel" and "Franchise Holder" and create two more subject data bases.

"Sleeping Accommodation," though shown as a separate subject data base, is actually a child of "Hotel" and will include "Hotel Identification" as part of the key for every record in it.

The expansion of each subject data base becomes completely dependent on the business functions it must serve in any specific application system. To illustrate this, let us consider a hotel customer system encompassing reservations, occupancy and charging for services. This example illustrates how the subject data bases are expanded. It further illustrates how the canonical model may be modified during application system design to increase processing efficiency. Later, we will use the same example to illustrate the operational planning phases and activities.

A HOTEL CUSTOMER SYSTEM

Function: To provide information on customer room reservations, occupancy and charges for services rendered.

This system consists of several applications identified during the information architecture phase (see Appendix A, Table 7) including:

06-01   Sleeping Accommodation
06-02   Meeting Banquet Rooms
07-02   Equipment Rental
14-03   Telephone Services
01-03   Accounts Receivable
12-01   Customer

The subject data bases created by these applications (Table 7.2) are:

8 Sleeping Accommodation
9 Meeting/Banquet Room
15 Equipment Data
17 Telephone Services
14 Financial
12 Customer

TABLE 7.2 Vacation
Hotels—Subject Data Bases
(Appendix A—Table 6)

---

8 *Sleeping Accommodation*
   Sleeping Accommodation
   Reservation
   Occupancy
   Charge
9 *Meeting/Banquet Rooms*
   Meeting Banquet Room
   Reservation
   Occupancy
   Charge
5 *Equipment*
   Equipment
     Equipment Reservation
     Equipment Rental
     Charge
     Inventory
17 *Telephone*
   Telephone
     Local
     Charge
     Long Distance
     Charge
14 *Financial Entities*
   Department (Cost Center)
     Transaction Type
     Charge
   Chart of Accounts
12 *Customer*
   Customer
     Reservation
     Accounts Receivable Invoice
     Charge

Let us examine and expand each of these subject data bases:

Sleeping accommodation (Table 7.3).   From the E-R diagram (Figure 6.2), we know that "Sleeping Accommodation" is a child of "Hotel." As reservations can be made through "Head Office," the "Hotel" key must be part of the "Sleeping Accommodation" key. We also know that hotel rooms are identified by a room number. So "Room Number" becomes part of the key. Rooms that are rented are divided into two groups, sleeping accommodation and meeting/banquet rooms, which have different features. An identifier is needed to distinguish between the two types. Let us call the "Sleeping Accommodation" identifier "Bedroom/Suite" and the "Meeting/Banquet Room" identifier, "M/B Room."

TABLE 7.3   Sleeping Accommodation (Appendix A, Table 12)

	03 SLEEPING ACCOMMODATION (*Hotel, Room No., Bedroom/Suite* Room Type, No. of Persons, Refrigerator, View)
	04 SLEEPING ACCOMMODATION RATE (*Hotel, Room No., Bedroom/Suite, Period* Single, Double, Additional Person)
Sleeping Accommodation/ Customer Relationship	05 S.A. RESERVATION (*Hotel, Room No., Bedroom/ Suite, Customer Id., Reserv. Ref.* Arrival Date, No. of Persons, Arrival Time, Departure Date, Payment Method)
Sleeping Accommodation/ Customer Relationship	06 S.A. OCCUPANCY (*Hotel, Room No., Bedroom/Suite, Customer Id., Occup. Ref.* Occup. Date, Rate Discount, No. of Persons)

As we want information on charging for services rendered, we need to establish a room rate. As this rate varies during different periods of the year, we establish a record called "Sleeping Accommodation Rate" which has "Period" as an additional identifier.

From the entities listed in the subject data base, we have two similar records called "Sleeping Accommodation Reservation" and "Occupancy." These were highlighted in the E-R diagram as possible relationship entities between the customer and the room. Hence, their keys include the "Customer Id." The keys for both records are identical and there is no way to distinguish between them. So, further identifiers are needed, for example, "Reservation Reference" and "Occupation Reference." Such reference numbers serve two functions: They distinguish between possible identical records and they provide the link to an accounting (general ledger) line item. We will refer back to this reference number when we discuss the "GL (General Ledger) Line Item" record. In most instances, such unique reference numbers can be used alone as the primary key, while the parent keys become foreign keys.

When a relationship entity is defined, expanded in a subject data base and entered in a data dictionary, there is no need to duplicate this effort in other subject data base(s) where this relationship entity occurs. Hence, the "Customer" subject data base will not include the expanded "Reservation" and "Occupancy" relationship entities.

The last entity listed in the "Sleeping Accommodation" subject data base was "Charge." (It should be noted that "Charge" is not shown in Figure 6.2, the E-R diagram, but is assumed for every service provided by the hotel. This charge becomes an accounts receivable item if the customer is to be invoiced). As "Charge" occurs frequently, it is best defined and expanded in the "Financial" subject data base. Further, as "Charge" and

"Advance" are identical and result in GL line items, they are renamed "GL Line Item."

Meeting/banquet room (Table 7.4).   This subject data base is almost identical to the preceding one and needs no further explanation.

TABLE 7.4   Meeting/Banquet Room (Appendix A—Table 12)

	07 MEETING/BANQUET ROOM (*Hotel, Room No., M/B Room* Room Type, No. of Persons, Features, View)
	08 MEETING/BANQUET ROOM RATE (*Hotel, Room No., M/B Room, Meal Income* M/B Room Rate)
Meeting/Banquet Room/Customer Relationship	09 M/B RESERVATION (*Hotel, Room No., M/B Room, Customer Id., Reserv. Ref.* Arrival Date, Time of Day, Departure Date, Payment Method, No. Attending, Table Type, Coffee Break, Lunch, Dinner)
Meeting/Banquet Room/Customer Relationship	10 M/B OCCUPANCY *Hotel, Room No., M/B Room, Customer Id., Occup. Ref.* Occup. Date, No. of Persons)

Equipment (Table 7.5).   From the viewpoint of the hotel customer system, we are only interested in equipment, equipment reservation and equipment rental. Both "Reservation" and "Rental" are relationship entities and link with "Customer."

TABLE 7.5   Equipment (Appendix A—Table 12)

	11 EQUIPMENT (*Hotel, Equipment Type* Rate, No. in Stock)
Equipment/Customer Relationship	12 EQUIP RESERVATION (*Hotel, Customer Id., Equipment Type, Reserv. Ref.* Room No., Reserv. Date, Time of Day, Number Reserved)
Equipment/Customer Relationship	13 EQUIP RENTAL (*Hotel, Customer Id., Equipment Type, Rental Ref.* Room No., Rental Date, Number Rented)

Telephone services (Table 7.6).   Telephone calls are made from rooms, hence "Room No." serves to identify the customer through the relevant occupancy record.

TABLE 7.6   Telephone Services (Appendix A—Table 12)

Telephone/Room Rel.	14 TELEPHONE CALL (*Hotel, Room No., No. Called, Tel. Ref.* Call Date, Time, Local/Long Distance, No. of Minutes)

Financial (Table 7.7).   The financial entities pertinent to the hotel customer system are expanded. These are "Department," "Transaction

Type," "GL Line Item" and "Chart of Accounts." The "GL Line Item" record is a relationship entity between any business transaction record associated with an advance paid or a charge made, the hotel and the chart of accounts. The logical pointer to the business transaction record is the "Business Transaction Reference" which has the same value as the reference in the particular record, for example, "Reservation Reference," "Occupation Reference," and so on. "GL Reference" is the general ledger reference number. It should be noted that the invoice number is added later to the GL line item when the invoice is produced.

In the "Financial" subject data base, we also have two independent entities listed: department (cost center) and chart of accounts. Again, we should reach a decision whether to retain them in a single subject data base or to create two separate subject data bases.

TABLE 7.7 Financial (Appendix A—Table 12)

	15 DEPARTMENT (*Hotel, Cost Center* Name, Function)
	16 TRANSACTION TYPE (*Hotel, Cost Center, Trans. Type* Description)
Transaction Type/COA Item/Business Transaction Relationship	17 GL LINE ITEM (*Hotel, Cost Center, Trans. Type, COA Item, Business Trans. Ref., GL Ref.*, Transaction Date, Advance/Charge, Invoice No.)

18 CHART OF ACCOUNTS ITEM (*COA ITEM No.* Item Description)

Note: 1. The transaction type indicates whether the transaction is budgeted or actual, and expense or income.

      2. The chart of accounts item identifies the account. Examples include:
- Sleeping Accommodation Reservation Advance
- Sleeping Accommodation Occupancy Charge
- Meeting/Banquet Room Reservation Advance
- Meeting/Banquet Room Occupancy Charge
- Equipment Charge
- Coffee Break Charge
- Meal Charge
- Telephone Call Charge
- Salary
- Overtime
- Benefits

The chart of accounts will probably be a hierarchy. Hence, the item no. will reflect the hierarchy levels. For example:

    08 Sleeping Accommodation
        01 Sleeping Accommodation Advance
        02 Sleeping Accommodation Charge

      3. The business transaction reference number has the same value as a reservation, occupancy, rental, and so on. Reference Number provides the link between GL line item record and the business transaction records.

Customer (Table 7.8).   The "Customer" subject data base includes the customer record which describes the customer. The credit card record has "Customer Id." as part of the key to identify which credit card the customer is using for payment of the account. "Customer Invoice" identifies the invoices issued to the customer.

TABLE 7.8   Customer (Appendix A—Table 12)

19 CUSTOMER (*Customer Id*. Name, Address, Company, Business Address, Home Phone, Business Phone)
20 CREDIT CARD (*Customer Id., Company Credit Card No.* Expiry Date)
21 CUSTOMER INVOICE (*Invoice No.* Invoice Date, Customer Id.)

Let's examine how these data can be used to produce invoice data for a hotel customer. We know the customer's name, room number, arrival date and at the end of the stay, the departure date. We also know whether a bedroom or a meeting/banquet room was occupied.

Invoice data are obtained by searching the reservation, occupancy, equipment, telephone, and other files by "Customer Id.," "Room No." and "Customer Arrival Date" to determine the business transaction references, which are then used to identify the GL line items.

In terms of displaying charge data or preparing an invoice, this procedure is inefficient because of the large number of data accesses needed to the different "service" type records. It could be made much more efficient by including "Customer Id." and "Room No." in the GL line item record. Then, only one file would be searched. Needless to say, these are redundant data from a canonical point of view.

TP2.2 Compare Subject Data Bases with Current Files and Documents

The data in the logical subject data bases are compared with current files and documents to identify entities and attributes which are not common. These entities and attributes are reviewed with the users to determine whether they should be included in the subject data bases or omitted.

This comparison serves as a control to ensure that all data currently available are reviewed in the context of the business needs at this point in time and for the planned future.

TP2.3 Normalize the Logical Subject Data Bases

The subject data bases should be normalized. Relationship entities need only be normalized in any one subject data base and entered in the data dictionary.

During application system design, it is very likely that more data attributes will be added to the records. When this occurs, the subject data bases should be normalized again.

The reader should note that the subject data bases found in Tables 7.2 to 7.7 were normalized as they were expanded, which is usually what happens when entity expansion is done. Activity TP2.3 then serves as a control to ensure that a canonical data model results.

TP2.4 Analyze the Data Distribution

Up to now, we have viewed data in logical terms and without regard to where the data should be stored and used. Large, centralized data storage systems may meet the needs of certain organizations but most organizations with branch plant or distributed operations require both decentralized data storage and data processing.

Data distribution and processing analysis is simple in principle but very complex in practice. Essentially, from the information and technical architecture phases of the strategic information resource plan, the distribution of business functions, subject data bases and applications are obtained. This information is expanded and analyzed in depth to determine which data are to be stored centrally, distributed and duplicated, the synchronization of data update, data extraction, and so forth.

The techniques involved in this analysis are beyond the scope of this book. However, many excellent references on the subject are available including James Martin's series on distributed processing published by Prentice-Hall, Inc.

TP3.1 List and Define the Physical Application Systems to Be Developed and Modified

The migration strategy phase of the strategic information resource plan provides a list of logical applications to be developed and current physical applications to be modified, with priorities established. These applications form the basis for the definition of physical applications to be developed or modified.

Individual physical applications may mirror logical applications, combine two or more logical applications, or be part of a logical application.

Each physical application must be defined and scoped in sufficient depth to enable the system to be designed, developed and implemented in the operational planning stage. This definition and scope must include the type of system, for example, batch, online, interactive or combinations of the different types; the subject data bases that are updated and used; the location of the data bases and whether they are duplicated; the degree of synchronization of data update, and the distribution of the application functions.

The technical architecture phase (SP3) of the strategic information resource plan and activity TP2.4 (analyze the data distribution) provides input to this activity.

8
The Information Resource Management Process: Operational Planning— System Specification and Procedure Design

STRIPE PHASES

OP2   Business System Specification

OP3   Procedure Design

Operational planning is directed at delivering products such as programs, files, reports and screens which will be used in production mode to meet business, data, application and technical needs. In this chapter, we view operational planning from the information resource management perspective and limit the discussion to system specification and procedure design. Table 8.1 highlights the outputs from system specification and procedure design. In Chapters 9 through 12, we convert these specifications and procedures into an implemented and maintainable application system.

The discussion to this point has been on a global scale in terms of data and application systems. We now view each application system and the subject data bases it updates or uses as a separate application set to be analyzed and defined.

Phase OP2 (Business System Specification) includes the expansion of functions to the lowest level to be included in any procedure, definition of the contents of all outputs and the design of the outputs. OP3 (Procedure

TABLE 8.1 The STRIPE Matrix Highlighting the Information Resource Management Outputs During Operational Planning

	Business	Data	Application	Technical Environment	Type of Plan
STRATEGIC PLANNING	SP1 Business Strategy: Mission Objectives and Goals Strategic Directions Critical Success Factors (CSFs) Major Information Requirements SP2 Major Functions (Processes) SP4 User and MIS Department Evaluation SP4 Proposed Organizations	SP2 Data Architecture: Primary Entities Crown E-R Diagram Subject Data Bases	SP2 Application Architecture: Business Applications SP4 Current Application Evaluation	SP3 Technical Architecture: Function Distribution Computers and Peripherals Data Distribution Communications Software (DBMS, Dictionary, Security) Office Automation SP4 Evaluation of Current Hardware/Software, Communications and Office Automation	SP4 Migration Plan: Major Projects over a 3–5 year period
TACTICAL PLANNING	TP1 Function Expansion TP1 ASDM Policy TP1 Organization Change: IRM Function Education Function Strategic Planning Function Quality Assurance	TP2 Logical Data Bases: Entity Expansion Current Files/ Documents Comparison Data Normalization Data Distribution	TP3 Physical Application Definition	TP4 Hardware/Software Communications/ Office Automation Specifications TP5 Selection of: Computers, etc. Communications Equipment Software Office Automation Equipment and Software	SP5 Budget Year Plan: (or similar period) Prioritized Projects scheduled and resourced
OPERATIONAL PLANNING	OP2 Business System Specifications: Activity Level Functions Output Requirements Output Design OP9 System Implementation: Manual Procedures D.P. Operations Procedures Education OP7 System Test: Testing OP10 System Review: Business Needs Operating Efficiency	OP4 Physical Data Base Design: Activity Level Data Expansion Data Volumes Data Accesses Physical Data Bases Physical DB Access Modules OP7 Testing OP9 File Conversion	OP3 Procedure Design: Event and External Action/Condition Analysis Embryonic Procedures Menu Hierarchies Input Screens and Forms OP5 Procedure Expansion: File Update Logic Output Logic OP6 System Construction: Physical Procedures OP8 Package Acquisition OP7 System Test: Testing OP9 Production Libraries	OP11 Product Implementation: Product Acquisition Product Installation Product Conversion Product Testing	OP1 Individual Project Plans

Design) includes data analysis and embryonic procedure definition. Functions here are restricted to business needs only. Program control and other programming functions are defined later during the design of the physical procedures in system construction discussed in Chapter 9.

In conventional application system design terms, we are now commencing definition of the business specifications. (Table 12.2 lists the phases and the outputs for a generic application systems development methodology). Should an organization either carry out all of the strategic and tactical planning phases of STRIPE or develop an information resource management framework, they could now commence system development using their own development methodology, if they so choose.

A further option available to the organization would be to modify Activity OP2.1 (Define Activity Level Functions) to develop process flows such as data flow diagrams (1) or Warnier/Orr diagrams (2&3). The end result should be the same, that is, the lowest-level functions within an activity.

8.1 OPERATIONAL PLANNING—SYSTEM SPECIFICATION

OP2.1 Define Activity Level Functions

The business functions associated with the application system being specified are expanded to the lowest level of data update within an activity. This level should provide all data (probably at the attribute level) to complete the expansion of every record in the subject data bases. Examples of such functions are "Reduce Stock," "Record Order" and "Update Receivable Balance." The logic to execute these functions are defined later during procedure expansion.

During procedure design in Activity OP3.1, all the basic functions identified here *must* be accounted for. It is possible that, in Activity OP3.1, additional functions may be identified.

OP2.2 Define Output Requirements

The users need data organized in the form of screens, reports, statements, checks, and so on to operate the business. This applies from the lowest worker to the most senior executive. Some forms of output are constant, particularly at the worker and middle-management levels, whereas senior management's needs change depending on the types of decisions to be made. All these data may be at both the record and the data attribute levels. The problem is to define the data required on each output.

Two sources of information for defining the data required on each output are the functions which have been defined in detail, and outputs currently in use. It is emphasized that this activity is intended to capture what data need to be displayed and not how the data are formatted. The formatting is done during the next activity.

OP2.3 Design the Output Formats

All output reports and screens are designed, preferably using screen painting of some form, so that the users can see what their output would be like when the system is in production.

This on-line designing of outputs with the users is commonly referred to as "prototyping of the outputs." Prototyping of the system design is much more comprehensive and includes designing the files or data bases, simulating the programs and testing the system to ensure that the business functions and data included in the system reflect the real business needs.

8.2 OPERATIONAL PLANNING—PROCEDURE DESIGN

Computer procedures can be designed using a variety of techniques such as Structured Analysis and Design (1,4&5), Data Structured System Design (2&3) and Information Engineering (6&7). The technique discussed here is based on data analysis in terms of the real-world happenings which cause data to change. I first introduced my view of this approach in *Information System Specification and Design Road Map* (8).

Data Maintenance and Update Concepts

Every system can be considered a black box which has input, process, files and output. The basic difference between a business system and a functional output system is that the majority of the business system's outputs are in the form of information (formatted data) printed in reports, invoices, screens, checks, and so on, while most functional outputs are not printed information. For example, an elevator system's output is to bring the elevator to the appropriate floor, a missile guidance system's output is to keep the missile on target and a traffic control system's output is to regulate the traffic lights to best fit the flow of traffic. Data input, data stored, data processed and data output can be drawn as shown in Figure 8.1A.

The conventional approach to information system design, regardless of

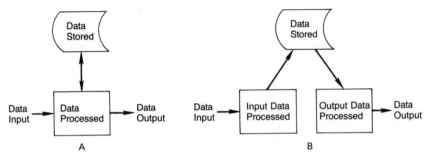

Figure 8.1 Input—Process—Output

the technique, is that data are input to a process which reads data stored in files, updates the files and produces the data output. By implication, data can be output from the process which do not have to be recorded in any file. For example, a program or module could have a table of data element values embedded in it. Such data are integral to the process, and the data and process cannot be separated. These data are called *internal variables*. Such systems are usually difficult to maintain because a change in program logic could change or lose internal variables. This could result in a chain reaction through other programs or modules causing totally unexpected problems. What is even worse with internal variables is that there is no audit trail to follow through the files.

To overcome this problem, systems can be designed so that inputs *only* update files and files *only* produce outputs. (*File* implies production files only and excludes files which spool reports and other outputs before printing them.)

Now we have five components in a basic computer system: data input, data input processed, data stored, data output processed and the data output. See Figure 8.1B. The distinction between the data input processed and the data output processed enables us to look at system design in two parts: file maintenance and output production.

File maintenance.   File maintenance is the processing of input data to update the data stored in the files. (The term *file* includes data base management systems.) The programs maintain each stored record individually. Each input record's content and structure are read and matched with the record definition in the program or data base management system. If it does not match the record definition, it will be rejected. If it matches the record definition, it could be further validated with criteria included in the program. Assuming that it is a valid record, it may then update a record in file or combine with other input data and/or records in file and update another record.

Human readable output data obtained during file maintenance should relate only to information regarding acceptance or rejection of the input data. (These output data are not to be confused with the data obtained during output production).

The basic functions performed during file maintenance are:

- the addition of records;
- the deletion of records;
- the modification of records (the addition, deletion or the updating of data attributes);
- the reading (accessing) of data in a record without updating it.

These additions, deletions, modifications and data accesses are called function events. (*Event* is a term coined by Clive Finkelstein to describe a basic or low-level function within a procedure (6). It is not to be confused with "events" in the real world which are referred to in this discussion as "actions" or "conditions".) The following example illustrates these function events.

An orders file contains the following records. (Keys are underlined):

- Customer (Customer Number, Customer Name, Customer Address)
- Order Header (Order Number, Customer Number)
- Product (Product Number, Product Name, Product Price, Quantity in Stock)
- Order Item [line item in the order] (Order Number, Item Number, Product Number, Quantity Ordered)

When an order for stock is received, the basic function events that occur are:

- The customer record input is validated. (Customer is read.)
- An invalid customer record is rejected.
- An order header record is set up. (Order Header is added.)
- The product ordered is validated. (Product is read.)
- An invalid product is rejected.
- An order item is set up. (Order Item is added.)
- The stock is verified. (Product is read.)
- The stock is reduced. (Product is modified.)

It could be concluded from this example that in file maintenance, highly functional modules can be designed where each module executes a single, basic function event, for example, add, delete, modify or retrieve records. The only additional functions these modules should be designed to perform are the necessary validations and computations required to update a particular record. Other functional modules to handle external interfaces such as "enter," "exit," "print," and so forth, are added to complete the procedure.

Later, during system construction when the program is being coded, more detailed functions to manipulate the data, the files, the screens, and others will be used. The complexity of these instructions will depend on the type of programming language, code generator or data base management system in use.

Output production.   In output production, programs take data (without removing or changing them) from a file or files and produce reports such as video screens, invoices, checks, control reports and files. These latter files could be input to other file maintenance or could be printed.

Referring back to the order example, the order could be printed with the order header and several line items, or a list of stock reductions could be produced.

It is worth emphasizing that by dividing the data processed into file maintenance and output production, the updating of the files has been completely separated from the production of output. Also, the production of reports during one output production process is completely independent of every other similar output production process.

Before the reader concludes that file maintenance and output production must always be in separate programs, it should be noted that a program may contain both features. What is essential is that the modules within the program not combine the two features. This is illustrated using our order example:

File Maintenance
1. Add ORDER HEADER   Read ORDER HEADER record input
    includes validation of   Validate CUSTOMER NUMBER
    CUSTOMER NUMBER   Reject invalid CUSTOMER NUMBER
                              Establish ORDER HEADER
                              Read ORDER ITEM record input

2. Add ORDER ITEM   Validate PRODUCT NUMBER
    includes PRODUCT   Reject invalid PRODUCT NUMBER
    validation and verifi-   Verify QUANTITY IN STOCK greater than
    cation of STOCK   QUANTITY ORDERED
    QUANTITY   Reject if insufficient QUANTITY IN
                                  STOCK
                              Establish ORDER ITEM

File Maintenance (cont.)

3. Modify QUANTITY IN   Reduce QUANTITY IN STOCK
   STOCK   Repeat Read of ORDER ITEM record until
                            no more ORDER ITEMS

Output Production

4.   Retrieve CUSTOMER NAME and CUS-
                            TOMER ADDRESS (from CUSTOMER
                            Record)
                            Print ORDER HEADER
                            Retrieve PRODUCT NAME and PROD-
                            UCT PRICE (from PRODUCT record)
                            Compute TOTAL PRODUCT COST
                            Print ORDER ITEM
                            Compute ORDER COST
                            Print ORDER COST
                            Compute TAX 7% of ORDER COST
                            Print TAX
                            Compute TOTAL ORDER COST
                            Print TOTAL ORDER COST

This program has two distinct parts: file maintenance and output production. The file maintenance consists of a series of modules which execute add, read and modify function events combined with validations and computations. The output production is one module which produces the report.

The first module establishes (adds) the "Order Header" record. To do this, it validates the "Customer Number." The second module establishes (adds) the "Order Item." To do this, it validates the "Product Number" and verifies that the "Quantity in Stock" is greater than the "Quantity Ordered." The third module reduces (modifies) the "Quantity in Stock." The fourth module produces a report.

To summarize, basic functions performed during file maintenance and output production are called function events. These function events can be divided into five classes:

1. Basic Maintenance (add, delete and modify records)

2. Access (read or retrieve records)

3. Validate (validate records)

4. Algorithmic (compute or execute an algorithm to change the value of a data element)

5. External interfaces (enter, obtain, exit, print, and so on)

Only add, delete and modify function events can update data in a file.

Read or retrieve function events can access data in a file but do not change it. So, if function events were considered to be building blocks, the basic maintenance function events would be the foundation. The access function events would be the second layer, the validate and algorithmic function events would be the third layer and the external interfaces would be the topmost layer.

Procedure Design Concepts

External actions or conditions identify specifically when records are added, deleted, modified or retrieved. Let us look at an example. A customer walks into a bank and opens an account. This sets in progress a chain of events which results in several new records being established. Similarly, when someone closes an account or dies, another chain of events is triggered which results in some records being deleted and others being modified. The same thing happens when money is deposited or withdrawn, a check is signed or a loan is taken. If each of these records were to be analyzed in terms of the function events which add, delete, modify or access them, all these external actions or conditions could be identified.

In the orders program example, the procedure consists of function events which occur "when" *an order for stock is received.*

We can conclude that every real-world action or condition can result in a procedure and that this procedure can be broken down into logical function modules which add, delete or modify records, and modules to produce output reports.

How do we capture this information? The tools used are called event and condition tables. To understand their use, let us return to the hotel example.

Event and condition tables.   An event table is used to analyze records in terms of record additions, deletions and modifications, and link them to the external actions or conditions which trigger them. The column headings in the event table (Table 8.3) are: "Dynamic," "Record Name," "Data Element," "Event Number," "Event Description," "Action/Condition Number," and "Comments." *Dynamic* is another term coined by Clive Finkelstein (6) to code record addition "A," deletion "D" or modification "M." The "Data Element" column lists the data elements associated with the function event. To illustrate, in Table 8.2, "Name," "Address" and

TABLE 8.2   Hotel Subject Data Base (Appendix A—Table 12)

01 HOTEL (*Hotel Id.* Name, Address, Location, Telephone No., Telex No., No. of Bedrooms, No. of Meeting/Banquet Rooms, Hotel Open/Closed)

02 ROOM (*Hotel, Room No.* Area)

"Location" are added or deleted when the hotel record is added or deleted. "Telephone Number" can change and becomes a modification of the record. The "Action/Condition Number" is the reference to the action or condition which triggers the occurrence of the event. (The action/condition is listed in the condition table, Table 8.4). The "Comments" column is used to provide additional information about the event such as an "if" to be included in the algorithmic process.

Other columns that could be included in the event table but not shown in the example are the "Physical Module Reference" and the "Physical Data Storage Reference." This information should be added later during the system construction process.

A condition table (Table 8.4) is used to identify the external (outside the computer system) actions or conditions which trigger data change and to link them to the function events which change the data. The condition table contains the same data as the event table except that it is sequenced by condition.

A single action or condition can trigger several function events and one function event can be triggered by more than one action or condition. The function events associated with a single action or condition make up an

TABLE 8.3 Event Table (Appendix A—Table 13)

Dynamic	Record Name	Data Element	Event Number	Event Description	Action/ Condition Number	Comment
A	Hotel	Name Address Location	01	Establish Hotel Rec.	01	—
D	Hotel	Name Address Location	02	Delete Hotel Record	02	—
M	Hotel	Telephone Number	03	Change Telephone Number	03	—
M	Hotel	Telex No.	04	Change Telex Number	04	—
M	Hotel	No. of Bedrooms	05	Change No. of Bedrooms	05	—
M	Hotel	No. of M/B Rooms	05a	Change No. of M/B Rooms	05	—
M	Hotel	Hotel open/closed	06	Change Hotel Status	06 01	—
A	Room	Area	08a	Establish Room Rec.	01	—
D	Room	Area	08b	Delete Room Rec.	06	—

Note: Event tables could include the physical module and physical data storage references.

embryonic procedure. The condition table also identifies the application which updates the procedure, and the organizational group responsible for executing the procedure.

The column headings in the condition table are "Update Application," "Action/Condition Number," "Action/Condition Description," "Dynamic," "Event Number," "Event Description" and "Organization Group Responsible."

It is strongly recommended that as the data are analyzed, the event and condition tables be entered into a data base management system or data dictionary which can execute relational "joins". Such software will permit easy maintenance of function event and action/condition data, as well as provide reports combining function event and action/condition information.

This system design technique is well suited to the design of interactive on-line systems because each procedure is dependent on some real-world action or condition occurring.

Hotel Subject Data Base Analysis

The hotel subject data base (Table 8.2) contains two records, "Hotel" and "Room," in canonical (third normal) form. Let us analyze these records in terms of the addition, deletion and modification function events and complete the event (Table 8.3) and condition tables (Table 8.4). A hotel record is established (Event 01) when a new hotel is opened (Condition 01). A hotel record is deleted (Event 02) when information on a closed hotel is no longer required (Condition 02). The "Name," "Address" and "Location" attributes of "Hotel" are entered or deleted when the hotel record is established or deleted. Note that the primary key data element, "Hotel Id.," need not be recorded in the "Data Element" column, as the addition or deletion of any record in a file implies the entry or removal of the key.

The addition, change in value or deletion of "Telephone Number" (Event 03) is dependent on the telephone number being changed (Condition 03). It could be argued that a telephone number cannot be changed unless it is there. If such arguments crop up, as they most certainly will, word the condition statement to take care of both contingencies. Condition 03 could then become "Add/Change Telephone Number." The remaining data attributes in the hotel record and the room record are analyzed in the same way.

In the condition table, we find that when a new hotel is opened (Condition 01), six new records are added. Similarly, when a hotel is closed (Condition 06), one record is modified (the "Hotel Status" is changed) and three records are deleted. Each of these conditions becomes a potential interactive on-line procedure.

Associated with this procedure, output reports may be produced. These outputs are also treated as function events and added to the procedure.

TABLE 8.4 Condition Table (Appendix A—Table 14)

Update Application	Action/ Condition Number	Action/ Condition Description	Dynamic	Event Number	Event Description	Organization Responsible
4.2 Franchise Management Accounting Administration	01	When new hotel opened	A	01	Establish Hotel Rec.	Head Office
			A	08a	Establish Room Rec.	
			A	09	Estab. Sl. Ac-commo. Rec.	
			A	12	Estab. Sl. Ac-commo. Rate Record	
			A	29	Estab. Meet./ Banquet Room Record	
			A	32	Estab. Meet./ Banquet Room Rate Rec.	
	02	When information on closed hotel is no longer required.	D	02	Delete Hotel Record	
	03	If hotel telephone no. changed	M	03	Change Teleph. No.	

04	If hotel telex no. changed	M	04	Change Telex Number
05	If hotel expanded	M	05	Change No. of Bedrooms
		M	05a	Change No. of M/B Rooms
		A	09	Estab. Sleep. Accommo. Rec.
		A	29	Estab. Meet./Banquet Room Record
06	If hotel closed	M	06	Change Hotel Status
		D	08b	Delete Room Record
		D	10	Delete Sleep. Accommo. Rec.
		D	13	Delete Sleep. Accommo. Rate Record

These basic function events must be expanded in Activity OP5.1 to include data retrieval, data validation and algorithmic logic. External interfaces (enter, obtain, exit, print, and so on) must also be added.

Update and output production procedures should have menu structures above them to provide easy and immediate access to them as needed. These menus are designed in Activity OP3.3 which is discussed in the next chapter.

Which application owns this procedure? From the information architecture, we know which subject data bases belong to particular applications. In most instances, the procedures resulting from the function event analysis of the records in the subject data bases would also belong to the same application. Occasionally, the procedure may belong to some other application. When this occurs, the particular application should be obvious.

Identifying the organization group responsible for executing the procedure may be straightforward or could be complicated by several groups being eligible. If the latter were to occur, it would point out replications of similar functions in different departments, which in turn could trigger reallocation of responsibilities or even reorganization of functions and staff. The activities to execute data analysis and procedure design follow.

OP3.1 Analyze Function Events and External Actions/Conditions

For each subject data base updated by the application system being developed, every record and data attribute are analyzed in terms of the basic function events, that is, data additions, deletions and modifications, and the real-world actions or conditions which trigger them. Event and condition tables are developed from the analysis.

A particular function event can be triggered by one or more real-world actions or conditions. Conversely, several function events could be triggered by a single action or condition.

All functions defined in Activity OP2.1 *must* be accounted for during this analysis. However, this analysis may result in more functions being identified than were defined in Activity OP2.1.

It is good practice to create the event and condition tables concurrently. A further suggestion is to include columns in the event table to cross-reference the physical program modules which are developed from the function events and to indicate where the module is physically stored.

OP3.2 Define Procedures

Each action or condition is converted into a separate procedure. Further function events are added to produce outputs associated with the procedure. The application system is identified in the procedure and the organization group responsible for the procedure is named.

REFERENCES

1. Tom DeMarco, *Structured Analysis and System Specification* (Englewood Cliffs, NJ: Prentice-Hall, Inc., 1979), copyright © 1978, 1979 Yourdon, Inc.
2. Kenneth T. Orr, *Structured Systems Development* (New York: Yourdon Press, 1977).
3. Kenneth T. Orr, *Structured Requirements Definition* (Topeka, KS: Ken Orr and Associates, Inc., 1981).
4. Edward Yourdon and Larry Constantine, *Structured Design* (Englewood Cliffs, NJ: Prentice-Hall, Inc., 1979).
5. Chris Cane and Trish Sarson, *Structured Systems Analysis: Tools and Techniques* (Englewood Cliffs, NJ: Prentice-Hall, Inc., 1979).
6. Clive Finkelstein, six articles on information engineering, *Computerworld,* May 11 to June 15, 1981.
7. James Martin and Clive Finkelstein, *Information Engineering* (Savant Research Studies, 2 New Street, Carnforth, Lancashire, LA5 9BX, England, 1981).
8. Denis Connor, *Information System Specification and Design Road Map* (Englewood Cliffs, NJ: Prentice-Hall, Inc., 1985).

9
Operational Planning: System Design and Development

STRIPE PHASES

OP3   Procedure Design
OP4   Physical Data Base Design
OP5   Procedure Expansion
OP6   Procedure Construction
OP7   System Testing

In Chapters 9 through 12 we convert the specified application system and the related subject data bases into physical applications and data bases which are implemented and put into production. In this chapter, we discuss all the STRIPE activities associated with system design and development. These are menu and input design from OP3 Procedure Design, OP4 Physical Data Base Design, OP5 Procedure Expansion, OP6 System Construction and OP7 System Test. These are highlighted in the STRIPE matrix in Table 9.1. These phases equate to the conventional system development methodology phases of system design, construction and testing listed in Table 12.2.

TABLE 9.1 The STRIPE Matrix Highlighting the System Design, Development and Testing Outputs During Operational Planning

	Business	Data	Application	Technical Environment	Type of Plan
STRATEGIC PLANNING	SP1 Business Strategy: Mission, Objectives and Goals, Strategic Directions, Critical Success Factors (CSFs), Major Information Requirements; SP2 Major Functions (Processes); SP4 User and MIS Department Evaluation; SP4 Proposed Organizations	SP2 Data Architecture: Primary Entities, Crown, E-R Diagram, Subject Data Bases	SP2 Application Architecture: Business Applications; SP4 Current Application Evaluation	SP3 Technical Architecture: Function Distribution, Computers and Peripherals, Data Distribution, Communications, Software (DBMS, Dictionary, Security), Office Automation; SP4 Evaluation of Current Hardware/Software, Communications and Office Automation	SP4 Migration Plan: Major Projects over a 3–5 year period
TACTICAL PLANNING	TP1 Function Expansion; TP1 ASDM Policy; TP1 Organization Change: IRM Function, Education Function, Strategic Planning Function, Quality Assurance	TP2 Logical Data Bases: Entity Expansion, Current Files/Documents Comparison, Data Normalization, Data Distribution	TP3 Physical Application Definition	TP4 Hardware/Software Communications/Office Automation Specifications; TP5 Selection of: Computers, etc., Communications Equipment Software, Office Automation Equipment and Software	SP5 Budget Year Plan: (or similar period) Prioritized Projects scheduled and resourced
OPERATIONAL PLANNING	OP2 Business System Specifications: Activity Level Functions, Output Requirements, Output Design; OP9 System Implementation: Manual Procedures, D.P. Operations Procedures, Education; OP7 System Test: Testing; OP10 System Review: Business Needs, Operating Efficiency	OP4 Physical Data Base Design: Activity Level, Data Expansion, Data Volumes, Data Accesses, Physical Data Bases, Physical DB Access Modules; OP7 Testing; OP9 File Conversion	OP3 Procedure Design: Event and External Action/Condition Analysis, Embryonic Procedures, Menu Hierarchies, Input Screens and Forms; OP5 Procedure Expansion: File Update Logic, Output Logic; OP6 System Construction: Physical Procedures; OP8 Package Acquisition; OP7 System Test: Testing; OP9 Production Libraries	OP11 Product Implementation: Product Acquisition, Product Installation, Product Conversion, Product Testing	OP1 Individual Project Plans

9.1 MENU AND INPUT DESIGN

A measure of successful interactive on-line systems is the ease with which the user can access the particular procedure (set of logical instructions) needed either by stepping through a series of menus similar to a table of contents, or by calling the particular procedure directly.

Using a data analysis approach to combine external actions or conditions with data update or access, we arrive at both the lowest-level procedures and their functional modules. We also know which applications own which procedures and the organizational groups responsible for executing them. All that remains is to build a menu hierarchy above these procedures to provide easy access to them, and to design the input screens to enter data into the system.

In batch systems, the menus are replaced by "manager" modules at different levels and the data are input through files instead of screens.

OP3.3 Design Menu Hierarchies

We can build menus in two ways: In the first, major functions and applications are emphasized, for example, an application lists all procedures and all organizational groups responsible for these procedures. So, a user has access to all other organizational groups' procedures. The function menu hierarchy could be set up as follows:

1 Function
2 Application
3 Procedure Group
4 Procedure
5 Function Event Module
6 Input Screens and Reports

In the second way, procedures specific to organizational groups are isolated. The organizational level menu would have one more level included:

1 Organization Group
2 Function
3 Application Specific to Organization Group
4 Procedure Group
5 Procedure Specific to Organization Group
6 Function Event Module
7 Input Screens and Reports

The second approach is much costlier than the first for two reasons: First, the functional set of menus must be designed, at least from a logical viewpoint, before the organizational set can be extracted. Second, a different set of menus must be built for each organizational group compared with a single set using the functional approach. We discuss both methods here.

How menus function.   The highest-level menu that can be accessed appears when the user logs on to the terminal or microcomputer. Each item on this menu is identified by a code, such as a letter of the alphabet or a numeric. The user can either enter the code in the block provided or can move the cursor to the particular item on the menu and press the "Return" key. This calls up the menu at the next level down and displays it. The user continues to do this until the procedure (set of instructions) is arrived at that he or she wishes to execute. Should the user wish to bypass the different menu levels, he or she can key in a string of menu codes and call up this procedure immediately.

Each screen is a module or set of computer instructions which needs to be designed and coded. Most data base management systems and fourth generation languages provide a facility such as a "dialogue manager" which greatly simplifies the development of these menus.

In the hotel example, we will use a two-digit number to identify each level with different menu levels separated by a period, with one exception: We will identify each organizational group using a letter of the alphabet.

Functional menu structures.

Menu Level 1—Function.   Fourteen functions ranging from 01 Finance to 14 Administration are listed (Table 9.2).

TABLE 9.2 Menu Hierarchy Based
on Function (Appendix A—Table 15)

Menu Level 1—Function
01   Finance
02   Marketing
03   Hotel Construction
04   Franchise Management
05   Franchise Sales
06   Room Reservations and Occupancy
07   Equipment Management
08   Recreation
09   Shop Management
10   Restaurant Management
11   External Services
12   Customer
13   Vendor
14   Administration

Menu Level 2—Application. Application systems are identified within each function. For example, in Function 01—Finance, the applications are 01 Budget, 02 Payroll, and so forth (Table 9.3).

TABLE 9.3 Menu Hierarchy Based on Function (Appendix A—Table 16)

Menu Level 2–Application

Function—01   Finance

01	Budget
02	Payroll
03	Accounts Receivable
04	Accounts Payable
05	General Ledger
06	Investments
07	Cash Management
08	Purchasing
09	Staff Pensions
10	Tax Tables

Function 04—Franchise Management

01	Quality Control
02	Account Administration
03	Building and Site Maintenance
04	Productivity Measurement

Menu Level 3—Procedure Group. Within each application system, four basic procedure groups are identified (Table 9.4). These are:

01   External Actions/Conditions
02   Records Created (Updated)
03   Records Used (Accessed) but Not Created (Updated)
04   Outputs

TABLE 9.4 Menu Hierarchy Based on Function (Appendix A—Table 17)

Menu Level 3—Procedure Group

Application 04.02 Franchise Management—Account Administration

01	External Actions/Conditions
02	Records Created (Updated)
03	Records Used (Accessed) but Not Created (Updated)
04	Outputs

01 External Actions/Conditions are the procedures identified during data analysis. They can include the updating of records and the production of outputs either on the screen or hardcopy. Because of the relative simplic-

ity of the hotel example, external actions/conditions are shown here as one level only. In more complex systems, it is very likely that several menu levels may be needed between the procedure group level and the actual procedure.

Procedure Groups 02, 03 and 04 should normally be accessed through a data dictionary or encyclopedia, as they are used to call up the data bases and the outputs defined in the dictionary. They are intended to provide easy access to the records and the outputs without using the external action/ condition procedures.

02 Records Created/Updated provides access directly to the records in file. The records listed should include only those created/updated by the specific application. Access to these records should be restricted to the group responsible for updating these records.

03 Records Used (Accessed) but Not Created provides "read only" access to the records in file used by the specific application.

04 Outputs are the screens, reports, and so on produced by the application.

Menu Level 4—Procedure Group—External Actions/Conditions.   To illustrate access to this menu level, let us examine the 04-02 Franchise Management—Account Administration application (Table 9.5).

TABLE 9.5   Menu Hierarchy Based on Function (Appendix A—Table 18)

Menu Level 4—Procedure

Application 04.02 Franchise Management—Account Administration

Procedure Group 04.02.01—External Actions and Conditions

01	When new hotel opened
02	When information on closed hotel is no longer required
03	If hotel telephone number is changed
04	If hotel telex number is changed
05	If hotel is expanded
06	If hotel is closed
16	When sleeping accommodation is no longer required by law
26	When meeting/banquet room occupancy information is no longer required by law
91	Annually

Following data analysis, we identified the applications and the procedures within each application. Each of these procedures executes functional modules to update or access data, and to produce outputs.

Entering 04.02.01 brings up the external actions/conditions procedure group and lists the procedures directly or the hierarchy (involving more levels). In account administration, we have only one level. On this screen, 04.02.01.01 identifies "when new hotel opened"; 04.02.01.02 identifies "when information on closed hotel is no longer required," and so forth.

Menu Level 5—Procedure.   Entering 04.02.01.01 (Table 9.6) brings up procedure "when new hotel opened" and lists the function event modules for this procedure.

TABLE 9.6   Menu Hierarchy Based on Function
(Appendix A—Table 19)

Menu Level 5—Function Event Module

Application 04.02 Franchise Management—Account Administration

Function Event Module 04.02.01.01—When new hotel opened

01	Establish hotel record
08a	Establish room record
09	Establish sleeping accommodation record
12	Establish sleeping accommodation rate
29	Establish meeting/banquet room record
32	Establish meeting/banquet room rate

Menu Level 6—Function Event Module.   Entering 04.02.01.01.01 (Table 9.7) brings up the input screen update module "establish hotel record."

TABLE 9.7   MENU HIERARCHY BASED ON FUNCTION (Appendix A—Table 20)

Menu Level 6—Input Screens and Reports

Application 04.02 Franchise Management—Account Administration

```
04.02.01.01.01   HOTEL

Hotel Identification Number _____

Hotel Name _____

Address _____

       _____

       _____

       _____

Location _____

Telephone Number _____

Telex Number _____

Number of Rooms _____

Hotel Open/Closed _____
```

Organizational group menu structure.   In the functional menu structure, we identified a minimum of six menu levels. With organization group menus, we add one more level at the top. In the hotel example, we identify this level using a letter from the alphabet. This eliminates confusion that may arise between the function and organization menus using a two-digit number.

The only difference between the two types of menu structures is that all data in the organization menu structure are confined to the particular organization group. For completeness, a separate menu structure must be set up for each organization group affected by a particular application.

In the hotel example, the organization level is:

A   Head Office
B   Hotel Administration
C   Sleeping Accommodation Administration
and so forth.

The functions level is:

A.01   Finance
A.02   Marketing
and so forth.

The main advantage of organization group menus is that the users have information that is relevant only to themselves on the screen. The disadvantage is that the effort involved in maintaining these menus is considerably more than that required for the function structure.

OP3.4 Design Input Screens and Forms

Input screens for interactive systems and forms for batch systems are designed to record data to be entered and subsequently used to update stored data. These screens and forms should be designed to meet the business needs rather than the system needs and may contain either single or multiple record data. Every procedure (driven by an action or condition) should have its own set of input screens.

9.2 PHYSICAL DATA BASE DESIGN

Physical data base design is done before procedure expansion and system construction are carried out. Procedure expansion must take into account all the data that have been previously defined in the physical data bases. A certain amount of iteration of all these activities can be expected as more information becomes known.

OP4.1 Expand Data to the Activity Level Functions

The data in the subject data bases are expanded to meet the needs of the lowest-level functions which have been defined in Activity OP2.1. This completes the definition of data based on function expansion. It may be necessary later to add programming control fields, such as flags, during system construction.

OP4.2 Confirm that Data to Provide the Outputs Identified in Activity OP2.2 Are Defined

Each defined output from Activity OP2.2 is systematically checked against the data defined in the subject data bases to confirm that the output can be produced from the stored data.

OP4.3 Analyze Data Usage in Terms of Volumes and Accesses

Information is needed to determine data storage needs for the system and to physically structure the data to obtain optimum efficiency. Data volumes are estimated based on record sizes and projected usage. Data paths will be dependent on data update and output production modules for each procedure. Iteration of data path analysis will occur later during physical procedure design.

OP4.4 Design the Physical Data Bases

Physical data bases may directly reflect individual subject data bases, combine two or more or be part of a particular subject data base. The structure of the physical data bases should be designed to conform as closely as possible to the logical subject data bases taking into account system efficiency. What should be guarded against is that a physical data base could become inflexible and unchangeable and require massive program changes, when alterations are needed to reflect changes made in the subject data bases.

The structure of the physical data base will be influenced by the characteristics of the data base management or file system in use, such as hierarchical, network, relational or flat file, and by the type and number of data accesses needed.

OP4.5 Design and Develop Data Base Access Modules

Data base access modules are needed to build a bridge between programs and data base management systems, particularly when the program language is not the data base management system's own update language. Building these access modules before designing and coding the physical programs makes the program design sin.pler, as these programs then only need to execute calls to the access modules.

9.3 PROCEDURE EXPANSION

OP5.1 Develop File Update Logic

The embryonic procedures defined in Activity OP3.2 are expanded to include logic for data validation, data base input/output, developing algorithms and external interfaces such as "enter," "exit," "print," and so on. In most business situations, this type of logic is straightforward. Complex situations can arise, however. The advantage of the functional module approach is that each attribute value to be changed can be determined independent of the other modules in the procedure.

OP5.2 Develop Output Logic

Output logic is defined to extract data from the data bases, manipulate them and present them on screens, reports, checks, and so on. When outputs are functions or graphics as in robotics or CAD/CAM, the logic becomes much more complex than with common business systems.

9.4 SYSTEM CONSTRUCTION

OP6.1 Design Physical Procedures

Physical program design is directed at obtaining the best mix of processing logic and operating efficiency. Physical programs could consist of one, two or more logical procedures combined to reduce file accesses, and so on. The design will be influenced by the programming language used because of the functions embedded in the language code. This activity includes all the logical procedures defined, such as file update, output production, menu structures and screen generation.

OP6.2 Code Physical Procedures

All processing logic is converted to program code. The quantity of code will depend on the type of language being used, for example, maximum for Assembler and minimum for a fourth generation language like SQL.

OP6.3 Test Physical Procedures

Test data are prepared for each physical procedure and each procedure is tested. Testing is iterative and could result in both code and procedure design changes.

9.5 SYSTEM TEST

Formal testing of the system is necessary even if prototyping techniques have been used for development. Testing must be done by the application developers to ensure that the system correctly updates the data stored and provides the outputs specified by the users. Testing must be done by the users to confirm that the system meets their business needs.

OP7.1 Prepare MIS and User Test Cases and Test Data

The application developers specify a series of test cases with accompanying test data to verify the operation of the system. The users prepare a corresponding set of test cases and test data to confirm that the functions of the system meet their business requirements. The application developers and users usually work together to prepare and execute the users' acceptance test of the system.

OP7.2 MIS Test System and

OP7.3 Users Test System

The system is tested first by the application developers and then by the users. Errors found can result in iteration of earlier activities and retesting.

10
Operational Planning: Application Package Acquisition

STRIPE PHASES

OP8   Application Package Acquisition

Companies generally decide to explore the acquiring of application packages instead of building applications in house when the functions are commonly used, such as financial applications, inventory management, project management, and others. The assumption made is that considerable savings in time and effort will result from the package acquisition. While this is often true, sometimes the problems associated with modifying and maintaining the package are equal to or exceed those associated with similar applications built in the company.

The activities associated with package acquisition are listed in Phase OP8. The output is highlighted in the STRIPE matrix in Table 10.1.

The decision to acquire a package covers three sets of criteria:

1. The degree of fit to the product requirements;

2. off-the-shelf versus turnkey packages; and

3. cost.

TABLE 10.1 The STRIPE Matrix Highlighting Application Package Acquisition During Operational Planning

	Business	Data	Application	Technical Environment	Type of Plan
STRATEGIC PLANNING	SP1 Business Strategy: Mission -Objectives and Goals Strategic Directions Critical Success Factors (CSFs) Major Information Requirements SP2 Major Functions (Processes) SP4 User and MIS Department Evaluation SP4 Proposed Organizations	SP2 Data Architecture: Primary Entities Crown E-R Diagram Subject Data Bases	SP2 Application Architecture: Business Applications SP4 Current Application Evaluation	SP3 Technical Architecture: Function Distribution Computers and Peripherals Data Distribution Communications Software (DBMS, Dictionary, Security) Office Automation SP4 Evaluation of Current Hardware/Software, Communications and Office Automation	SP4 Migration Plan: Major Projects over a 3–5 year period
TACTICAL PLANNING	TP1 Function Expansion TP1 ASDM Policy TP1 Organization Change: IRM Function Education Function Strategic Planning Function Quality Assurance	TP2 Logical Data Bases: Entity Expansion Current Files/ Documents Comparison Data Normalization Data Distribution	TP3 Physical Application Definition	TP4 Hardware/Software Communications/ Office Automation Specifications TP5 Selection of: Computers, etc. Communications Equipment Software Office Automation Equipment and Software	SP5 Budget Year Plan: (or similar period) Prioritized Projects scheduled and resourced
OPERATIONAL PLANNING	OP2 Business System Specifications: Activity Level Functions Output Requirements Output Design OP9 System Implementation: Manual Procedures D.P. Operations Procedures Education OP7 System Test: Testing OP10 System Review: Business Needs Operating Efficiency	OP4 Physical Data Base Design: Activity Level Data Expansion Data Volumes Data Accesses Physical Data Bases Physical DB Access Modules OP7 Testing OP9 File Conversion	OP3 Procedure Design: Event and External Action/Condition Analysis Embryonic Procedures Menu Hierarchies Input Screens and Forms OP5 Procedure Expansion: File Update Logic Output Logic OP6 System Construction: Physical Procedures OP8 Package Acquisition OP7 System Test: Testing OP9 Production Libraries	OP11 Product Implementation: Product Acquisition Product Installation Product Conversion Product Testing	OP1 Individual Project Plans

10.1 THE DEGREE OF FIT TO THE PRODUCT REQUIREMENTS

The information requirements that need to be defined to acquire a package are the same requirements that must be defined before an application is built. At the top of the list are the business functions the application must serve and the entities about which information must be provided. The functions are translated into procedures and processes, while the entities become records with keys and data attributes. The procedures should be defined both in terms of data maintenance and output production. These business specifications are compared in detail with the package's specifications.

Other requirements to be defined include:

- Does the business need an interactive or batch system, or a combination of both?
- Should the data be distributed or centralized? Must the package's files be stored using the company's data base management system? Will the package's data need to be renamed and reorganized to interface with the company's data?
- Would preformatted reports be sufficient or can the reports be customized?
- Does the package need to interface with other software, such as a general ledger package or a spreadsheet?

Access to the program code and the authority to modify or build interfacing programs should be taken into account. Most often, the package supplier will not permit access to source code and will provide only the object code to the customer. Whether the source code is modified or interfaces are built, this introduces a new set of complications because these additions will probably have to be rebuilt every time a new package release is issued.

Associated with the code is the language used. This language may not be in use in the organization. For example, the code is written in PL1 while the language used in house is COBOL.

10.2 OFF-THE-SHELF VERSUS TURNKEY PRODUCTS

Packages may be purchased off the shelf, be customized or be a combination of both. Completely customized packages, referred to as turnkey applications, are no different from those produced in house and suffer from the same problems. Off-the-shelf products which are customized may need to be customized every time a new release is issued. In general, off-the-shelf products which can be put to use without modification or interfaces being built are the best choice.

Products bought off the shelf should be well documented. The documentation should be easy to read and understand, and come with a detailed table of contents, index and glossary. The program documentation should include the logical processes, the actual source code, and a series of test cases. The file descriptions should provide detailed data definitions and the data structures.

Specifically, the quality of the data, the quality of the code, the simplicity of the code and whether it is structured or unstructured, the machine efficiency, and how closely the code resembles the logical processes should be evaluated.

Adequate education should be available either through supplier classroom courses or computer-aided education. Interactive packages should have a "help" facility which could be accessed every time the user has a need.

No matter how good the package, it is only as good as the supplier because if the supplier goes out of business, who will maintain the package? To assess the supplier, the number of years the company has been in business, the number of products sold and users' experience with the product should be taken into account. Further, what type of maintenance and service will be provided and have users' experiences been positive or negative? Users are generally very candid and provide strengths and weaknesses they have encountered. The exchange generally benefits both parties, as users may also gain useful information from you. It should also be considered whether the product can grow as new needs are identified.

Turnkey products, as stated earlier, are no different from products designed and built in house except that the design and development has been subcontracted. This may be done for several reasons, for example, resources or product expertise may not be available in house.

Turnkey products should satisfy the documentation requirements previously identified. Other questions that should be asked about turnkey products are: Who owns the product? Who maintains it? Who enhances it? What warranty will the supplier provide? Will the product have a fixed price or will its cost be based on the resources used to develop it?

10.3 COST

The cost of the package is not restricted to the price paid to the vendor. The cost includes:

* the cost of developing the specifications,
* the cost of customizing the package,
* the cost of installing updates to the package,
* the annual maintenance fee,

- the cost of conversion from the present system,
- the cost of writing off existing systems, and
- the cost of developing interfaces with other systems.

It is worth noting that the cost of developing the specifications would be incurred whether the application is built in house or a package is acquired, though possibly to a lesser degree as one of the reasons for purchasing a package could be to minimize the detailed specifications and design. All of these factors are hard costs and could be priced. Benefits are generally more difficult to cost because some are soft. These include:

- savings in development costs,
- more effective use of people and machine resources, and
- making use of vendor knowledge and experience not available in house.

11
Operational Planning: System Implementation and Review

OP9   System Implementation
OP10 System Review

This chapter completes the activities associated with building application systems. Implementation involves the establishment of the administration and controls needed which are external to the computer system. This includes items such as supplementary documentation, user education, program control libraries and file conversion (Phase OP9).

A system review is done after a system has been in production long enough (at least three months) to evaluate it in terms of meeting the business needs and its operating efficiency (Phase OP10). These STRIPE phases equate to similar phases in the conventional systems development methodology shown in Table 12.2. The outputs from these phases are highlighted in the STRIPE matrix in Table 11.1.

TABLE 11.1 The STRIPE Matrix Highlighting System Implementation and Review During Operational Planning

	Business	Data	Application	Technical Environment	Type of Plan
STRATEGIC PLANNING	SP1 Business Strategy: Mission Objectives and Goals Strategic Directions Critical Success Factors (CSFs) Major Information Requirements SP2 Major Functions (Processes) SP4 User and MIS Department Evaluation SP4 Proposed Organizations	SP2 Data Architecture: Primary Entities Crown E-R Diagram Subject Data Bases	SP2 Application Architecture: Business Applications SP4 Current Application Evaluation	SP3 Technical Architecture: Function Distribution Computers and Peripherals Data Distribution Communications Software (DBMS, Dictionary, Security) Office Automation SP4 Evaluation of Current Hardware/Software, Communications and Office Automation	SP4 Migration Plan: Major Projects over a 3–5 year period
TACTICAL PLANNING	TP1 Function Expansion TP1 ASDM Policy TP1 Organization Change: IRM Function Education Function Strategic Planning Function Quality Assurance	TP2 Logical Data Bases: Entity Expansion Current Files/ Documents Comparison Data Normalization Data Distribution	TP3 Physical Application Definition	TP4 Hardware/Software Communications/ Office Automation Specifications TP5 Selection of: Computers, etc. Communications Equipment Software Office Automation Equipment and Software	SP5 Budget Year Plan: (or similar period) Prioritized Projects scheduled and resourced
OPERATIONAL PLANNING	OP2 Business System Specifications: Activity Level Functions Output Requirements Output Design OP9 System Implementation: Manual Procedures D.P. Operations Procedures Education OP7 System Test: Testing OP10 System Review: Business Needs Operating Efficiency	OP4 Physical Data Base Design: Activity Level Data Expansion Data Volumes Data Accesses Physical Data Bases Physical DB Access Modules OP7 Testing OP9 File Conversion	OP3 Procedure Design: Event and External Action/Condition Analysis Embryonic Procedures Menu Hierarchies Input Screens and Forms OP5 Procedure Expansion: File Update Logic Output Logic OP6 System Construction: Physical Procedures OP8 Package Acquisition OP7 System Test: Testing OP9 Production Libraries	OP11 Product Implementation: Product Acquisition Product Installation Product Conversion Product Testing	OP1 Individual Project Plans

11.1 SYSTEM IMPLEMENTATION

OP9.1 Prepare Manual Procedures

User procedures to update and use the data stored are prepared. The users' manual procedures should be written as an extension to the computer procedures. The procedures shoud be supported by examples wherever possible with narrative text kept to a minimum. The ideal is matrices with specific procedures cross-referenced to responsibility centers, and matrices cross-referencing inputs and outputs to specific procedures.

OP9.2 Prepare Data Processing Operations Procedures

Operations department procedures to support on-line and batch systems are prepared. These operations procedures should have sufficient information in them to enable the data processing or operations staff to support and run the physical procedures for each application system.

OP9.3 Educate Users About the System

Training sessions for the system users are scheduled and given using the test cases developed earlier to illustrate the different system functions. The extent of the user training depends on a variety of factors such as their understanding of on-line and batch systems, the similarity of the new system to the one being replaced, the equipment being used, and so forth.

OP9.4 Establish Production Libraries for Physical Procedures

All test libraries are converted to production libraries. (It is assumed that the organization has software to manage all programs with version control.)

OP9.5 Convert Current Files

Current files/data bases are converted to the new file/data base structure. File or data base conversion can be very complex and be affected by the replacement of one data base management system with another, or with one supplier's hardware and related software with another. A conversion strategy should have been developed during the migration strategy phase of the strategic information resource plan which would provide the basis for the conversion. Different scenarios could be considered such as converting current files and data bases to the new data architecture as new systems are implemented; converting all existing files and data bases to the new data architecture and in the interim modifying the existing systems; maintaining the current files and data bases and building interfaces to the new files and data bases until the new systems are implemented, and so on.

Aside from the actual conversion problems, a major problem that may arise is the possibility that duplicate data base management systems and hardware from different suppliers, and related software could occupy expensive or unavailable space and thus double operating costs. If the organization is faced with such complex problems, file and data base conversion should be viewed as a separate major project outside of the implementation of the new data architecture and application systems.

11.2 SYSTEM REVIEW

OP10.1 Review Systems in Terms of Business Needs

The application system's functions and related data are reviewed in terms of the data stored and the outputs produced by the system to verify that the system meets the user's needs. If new functions are needed, these are added to the system and the data architecture is modified to include the new data needs. These modifications usually impact the production system, the physical data base structures and the production files or data bases.

The business review assures the user that the business functions are understood and satisfied through the data and application architectures.

OP10.2 Review Systems for Operating Efficiency

The system's performance is reviewed to determine what modifications, if any, need to be made to improve it. These modifications may seriously impact the logical data structure and the logical applications. A decision must then be made to live with poorer performance or to improve performance and accordingly increase the cost of adding system functions later on.

12
Prototyping Application Systems Development

This chapter describes how STRIPE can be used to prototype application systems development through iterative expansion and data analysis of the subject data bases, and how this prototyping approach compares with conventional systems development methodologies.

Figure 12.1 puts the information and technical architectures defined during development of the strategic information resource plan in perspective. The information architecture provides the data and application architectures. The technical architecture provides implementation options with regard to hardware, software, communications, office automation, and others for the whole organization. Hence, during development of individual business applications, the need to determine implementation options is not a concern. Emphasis can then be put on the design, development and implementation of individual applications.

Table 12.1 summarizes the STRIPE activities used to design and build application systems. The data and application system design phases are TP1 through to OP5. The system construction and test, system implementation and system review phases extend from OP6 to OP10.

How can we prototype using these STRIPE activities? The answer lies in the expansion of the subject data bases. The building of these data bases is dependent on the function level being analyzed. For example, at a very high

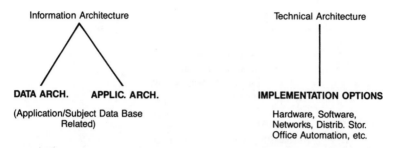

Figure 12.1   Strategic Information Resource Plan (SIRP) Level of System Design

function level, only the primary entities and possibly a few of the lower-level entities would be identified. These entities, in turn, would have few attributes. Using the data defined, preliminary output screens could be defined. Function event and action/condition analysis could next be done at this level and procedures defined, expanded, coded and tested.

Function expansion with consequent data expansion resulting in more data on the output screens could be continued. The cycle would be repeated until data expansion is complete and all procedures and screens are completely defined. In this way, the user could have exposure to the working system at different levels of detail until satisfied that the system is complete.

Even when the application is put into production, changes can still be made to the data structure and the procedures because each function event (record add, delete or modify) is highly functional and is either not dependent or only dependent in relation to time (when it occurs) on any other function event.

To obtain maximum advantage from this approach, all data, function events, actions/conditions, procedures, programs and modules should be defined in a data dictionary/directory which should also exert control over the design process; that is, no program or module should be changed without first working through the data structure, function event and action/condition analysis.

Let's compare this prototyping approach based on the information architecture with the generic application systems development methodology shown in Table 12.2. The first major difference is the elimination of the Phase 1 Feasibility Study. This study is not necessary because all business applications have been defined and approved during the information architecture phase of the strategic information resource plan (SIRP).

The second major difference is that Phases 2, 3 and 4, that is, the business specification, the system specification and the system design are iterated as functions are expanded and additional data are defined.

What are the benefits of the STRIPE prototyping approach to system development? The most important benefit is that the information architecture is part of the organization's strategic information resource plan and will

TABLE 12.1   Prototyping Using STRIPE

TP1	Function Expansion
TP2	Logical Data Base Design
	Subject Data Base Expansion
	Current Files/Documents Comparison
	Data Normalization
	Data Distribution
TP3	Physical Application Definition
OP2	Business System Specification
	Activity Level Functions
	Output Requirements
	Output Design
OP3	Procedure Design
	Function Event and External Action/Condition Analysis
	Embryonic Procedure Definition
	Menu Design
	Input Design
OP4	Physical Data Base Design
	Activity Level Data Expansion
	Data Volumes
	Data Accesses
	Physical Data Bases
	Physical Data Base Access Modules
OP5	Procedure Expansion
	File Update Logic
	Output Logic
OP6	System Construction
	Physical Procedure Code and Test
OP7	System Test
	Testing
OP9	System Implementation
	Manual Procedures Development
	User Education
	Production Program Libraries
	File Conversion
OP10	System Review
	Business Needs
	Operating Efficiency

change only when the organization's business changes. The second benefit is that the process of application system design and implementation becomes a dynamic and living thing which grows and changes as the business requirements grow and change. Systems can evolve as more information on system function and data become available. Finally, since the data bases are the sole source of output data, and the users have been heavily involved in developing the data architecture, they are in an excellent position to generate all nonproduction reports to meet their needs, using some form of report generator.

TABLE 12.2   A Generic Application Systems Development Methodology

Phase 1—*Feasibility Study*
  Project scope
  User's system objectives
  Performance requirements
  Interfacing systems
  General description of system to be developed with alternate choices
  Impact on the organization
  Impact on the computer environment
  Development cost
  Operating cost
  Benefits and risks

Phase 2—*Business Specification*
  Definition of the business objectives or the functions
  Definition of the data required to meet the objectives or the functions
  Definition of the logical records and files
  Definition of the data input
  Definition of the outputs (if required)
  Identification of when outputs or file data are required
  Identification of the need for centralized or decentralized files or data bases
  Definitions of the input process logic
  Definitions of the output process logic (if required)

Phase 3—*System Specification*
  Logical system divided into computerized and manual processes
  Possible implementation options such as on-line and batch update, on-line data access, etc. with their associated costs, benefits and estimated development schedules.

Phase 4—*System Design*
  Physical file or data base design
  Network design
  Physical architecture of subsystems and programs
  Detailed program and module logic
  Test plans
  File conversion plans
  Hardware and software acquisition and installation plans
  Implementation strategies

Phase 5—*Construction and Testing*

Phase 6—*System Implementation*

Phase 7—*System Review*

Glossary

The following definitions are intended to provide a common understanding of terms used in this textbook.

Application System An application system is a named set of related procedures or programs associated with the execution of a related set of business functions, such as accounts receivable.

Business Entity A business entity is something that exists in the real world outside the computer system. The computer system produces or uses information about it, for example, "Hotel," "Customer" and "Vendor." Entities have natural relationships based on the business rules and policies followed by the organization.

Business Function A business function can be defined as a particular kind of work (*Webster's New Collegiate Dictionary,* 1974). Functions can be both high and low level, such as manufacturing and machining. Manufacturing is viewed at the corporate level while machining is viewed at the job level.

Canonical Schema A canonical schema is a schema or data structure which has been normalized.

Canonical Synthesis Canonical synthesis is the development of a canonical schema through the sequential normalization of a series of user views (subschemas) of data.

Crown The Crown E-R diagram is the data model illustrating the primary or most important entities and their relationships in the organization. The crown can be considered to be the apex of the entity hierarchies and provides the essence of the business.

Data Base A data base is a data file which has defined logical and physical structures in which data are viewed and stored according to these structures. The logical structure is the view the user has of the structure and can be all or part of the data in a single physical data base or can cross physical data base boundaries. The physical structure is the way the data are actually organized and stored in a physical medium such as a disk file.

Data Element Data elements are defined in terms of the entity they are part of, a qualifier or descriptor, and a data type. The qualifier is the name given to the data element. The data type is the way the data element is recorded and is selected from a set of reserved words such as "Code," "Text," "Name" and "Amount." Examples of data elements are:

Entity	Qualifier	Data Type
Hotel	Hotel Name	Name
Invoice Line Item	Total	Amount
Product	Product Description	Text

Data Incompatibility Data incompatibility occurs when data are structured differently in different files requiring complex interfaces to pass data to and fro.

Data Inconsistency Data inconsistency occurs when multiple applications use the same data but with different names and shades of meaning.

Data Redundancy Data redundancy occurs when the same data are stored in different files, with the result that file updates do not occur simultaneously and information extracted from different files for different purposes contain different data.

Entity See *Business Entity*.

Entity-Relationship Diagram (E-R Diagram) An entity-relationship diagram is a data model illustrating the relationships between a set of entities reflecting the organization's business practices and policies through business rules.

Entity-relationship diagrams have only three types of entities: independent entities, dependent entities and relationships. An independent entity has no parent entity and its key is a single data element. For example, "Hotel" is an independent entity because it can be identified uniquely by a data element such as "Hotel Name" or "Hotel Identification Number." In a hierarchical data base, it would be the "root" or entry point.

A dependent entity has a parent entity and its key includes the parent entity key, for example, "Hotel Room."

HOTEL ROOM (*Hotel, Room Number,* Room Rate)

A relationship entity links two (or more) entities and includes the keys from these entities. However, these keys may or may not be part of the relationship entity key. Consider the following example:

BANQUET ROOM/ CUSTOMER Relationship	BANQUET ROOM RESERVATION (*Hotel, Room No., Customer Id., Reserv. Ref.* Arrival Date, Time of Day, Departure Date, Payment Method, No. Attending, Table Type, Coffee Break, Lunch, Dinner)

In this example, "Banquet Room" is linked to "Customer." Here the "Banquet Room" key and the "Customer" key together form part of the "Banquet Room Reservation" key. If a unique number could be given to the "Reservation Reference," then "Hotel," "Room Number" and "Customer Identification" would become attribute foreign keys.

Foreign Keys A foreign key is an attribute which is part or all of a key in another record. For example, a bill of lading is identified by the "Bill-of-Lading Number" and has among its attributes "Supplier," "Customer," "Product Shipped," "Source" and "Destination." All these attributes are keys from other records.

Intersection Data See *Relationship.*

Join A join occurs when data are combined from two or more records through a common field to produce a new record.

Key The key is that data element or set of elements which uniquely identifies a record. A single data element key is termed "simple." Multiple data element keys are termed "compound" when parent keys in a data hierarchy are included in the key to eliminate the dependency between the records. Keys are "concatenated" when the record results from a relationship between two independent entities. Examples of the three types of keys are:

Simple	Employee Identification Number
Compound	Employee Identification Number, Child Name The child cannot be identified except through the employee.
Concatenated	Employee Identification Number, Position Identification Number

"Employee" and "Position" are independent so that the employee's position is identified by a concatenated key made up of both "Employee" and "Position" keys.

Normalized Record In a normalized record, every descriptor (data attribute) is a fact about the whole key and nothing but the key. The normalization process results in the removal of interdependencies among data attributes.

Procedure A procedure is an instruction set which could be either manual or be performed by the computer.

Program A program is a computer procedure.

Projection A projection occurs where data are extracted from a record and restructured to produce a new record.

Record Entities become records which consist of fields or data elements. One or more data elements identify the record and are called the "key." The other data elements describe the record and are called "data attributes."

Relationship A relationship defines the association between two entities. Simple relationships do not become records, for example, a parent "has" children. Complex relationships often become records, for example, a "Flight" associates an airplane type with one or more airports. These complex relationship records are either identified by a concatenated key combining the entity keys or by including the entity keys as data attributes which are foreign keys. An example of the former is a "Hotel Reservation" whose key includes "Room Number" and "Customer Identification." An example of the latter is a "Flight" which is identified by a key called "Flight Number" and has among its attributes "Airplane Type" and "Airport."
A relationship can link several entities. For example, a "Bill of Lading" links "Supplier," "Customer," "Product," "Transportation Mode," "Source" and "Destination." Here bill of lading is identified by a unique "Bill-of-Lading Number" and the associated entities become foreign keys.
Note: *Relationship* is a term used by Peter Chen. James Martin uses the term *Intersection Data* instead.

Selection A selection occurs when particular instances of records are selected based on specific criteria.

Subject Data Base A subject data base is a logical data base relating to a clearly identifiable subject, which encompasses all or part of an entity family including specific relationship entities, for example, "Staff Data" in the Vacation Hotel case study.

APPENDIX A
Hotel Case Study Tables

Appendix A consists of a series of tables which illustrates the different examples drawn from the Vacation Hotel case study and described in the text. The textbook examples could be considered extracts from the detailed tables and provide only enough information to understand the point presented. The tables in the appendix are a complete expansion of the material and are intended to illustrate how the information would be represented in real life. The two sets of tables are cross-referenced so that the reader can go from the text to the detailed examples and vice versa.

APPENDIX A—TABLE 1 (TABLE 6.2)   Natural
Function Hierarchy

---

1 *Corporate Level*

Financial Services
  Accounts Receivable
  Accounts Payable
  General Ledger
  Investments
  Payroll
  Cash Management
  Budget
    Annual Budget Preparation
    Annual Budget Approval
    Annual Budget Implementation
      Monthly Budget Calendarization
      Monthly Budget Compared with Monthly Expenses
      Corrective Action

Marketing
  Sales
  Advertising
    Media
    Information Brochure

Hotel Construction
  Land Acquisition
  Architecture
  Planning
  Scheduling
  Obtaining Building Permits

Franchise Sales
  Planning
  Marketing

Franchise Management
  Account Administration
  Quality Control
  Building and Site Maintenance

Room Reservations and Occupancy
  Reservation
  Occupancy

Head Office Administration
  Human Resources (Personnel)
  Information Services
  Purchasing
  Inventory Control

2 *Hotel Level*

Financial Services
  Same as Corporate Level

Room Reservations and Occupancy
  Same as Corporate Level

APPENDIX A—TABLE 1 (TABLE 6.2) (*Continued*)

Equipment Management
  Inventory Control
  Equipment Rental
Recreation
  Recreation Facility Management
Shop Management
  Shop Rental
Restaurant Management
  Meal Planning
  Meal Preparation
  Entertainment
  Food Ordering
  Liquor Ordering
External Services
  Tour Arrangement
  Information Service
  Car Rental
Hotel Administration
  Same as Corporate Level
  Building Maintenance

APPENDIX A—TABLE 2 (TABLE 6.3) Capturing Functions and Entities

Functions	Entities
1 *Corporate Level*	
Financial Services	
Budget	Income
Accounts Receivable	Expenses
Accounts Payable	Profit
General Ledger	Assets
Investments	Tax
Payroll	Chart of Accounts Item
Cash Management	Cost Center
Marketing	
Sales	Location
Advertising	Hotel
Media	Accommodation
Information Brochure	Bedroom
	Meeting/Banquet Room
	Customer
	Vendor
	Restaurant
	Food
	Shop
	Recreation

APPENDIX A—TABLE 2 (TABLE 6.3) (*Continued*)

Functions	Entities
	Swimming Pool
	Golf
	Tennis
	Squash
	Gymnasium
	Other Sports
	External Services
	Guided Tour
	Airport Transport
	Public Transport
	Car Rental
Hotel Construction	
Land Acquisition	Plan
Architecture	Blueprint
Planning	Permit
Scheduling	Building Site
Obtaining Building Permits	Vendor
	Same as Marketing
Franchise Sales	
Planning	Franchise Holder
Marketing	Same as Marketing
Franchise Management	
Account Administration	Franchise Fee
Quality Control	Inspection
Building and Site Maintenance	Same as Marketing
Room Reservations and Occupancy	
Reservation	Bedroom
Occupancy	Meeting/Banquet Room
	Reservation
	Occupancy
	Customer
Head Office Administration	
Human Resources (Personnel)	Staff (Employee)
Information Services	Vendor
Purchasing	Equipment
Inventory Control	
2 *Hotel Level*	
Financial Services	
Same as Corporate Level	
Room Reservations and Occupancy	
Same as Corporate Level	
Equipment Management	
Inventory Control	Equipment
Equipment Rental	

APPENDIX A—TABLE 2 (TABLE 6.3) *(Continued)*

Functions	Entities
Recreation	
Recreation Facility Management	Equipment
	Schedule
	Reservation
Shop Management	
Shop Rental	Lease
	Rent
Restaurant Management	
Meal Planning	Menu
Meal Preparation	Meal
Entertainment	Bar
Food Ordering	Liquor
Liquor Ordering	Cutlery
	Crockery
	Furniture
External Services	
Tour Arrangement	Guided Tour
Information Service	Public Transport
Car Rental	Airport Transport
	Rented Car
Hotel Administration	
Same as Corporate Level	
Building Maintenance	Equipment
	Schedule

(Note: Functions and entities are listed as they are identified. Items on the same line do not imply separate dependencies. It should be emphasized that these are preliminary lists and can and will be added to as the design process continues.)

APPENDIX A—TABLE 3
(TABLE 6.4) Vacation Hotels—
Entity Hierarchy

Location
  Head Office
    Staff
      Salaries
      Benefits
      Pensions
      Education
      Work Schedules
    New Hotel Site
      Plans
      Blueprints
      Building Permits
      Construction

APPENDIX A—TABLE 3
(TABLE 6.4)   *(Continued)*

Hotel
  Franchise
    Franchise Fee
  Staff
    Salaries
    Benefits
    Pensions
    Education
    Work Schedules
  Hotel Inspections
  Equipment
    Equipment Reservations
    Equipment Rental
      Charge
    Inventory
  Maintenance
    Laundry
      Work Schedules
    Room Cleaning
      Work Schedules
    Other
      Work Schedules
  Recreation
    Swimming Pool
    Games
      Tennis
        Game Reservation
      Golf
        Game Reservation
      Other
        Game Reservation
    Gymnasium
  Restaurants
    Bar
      Charge
    Coffee Shop
      Meals
        Charge
    Dining Room
      Meals
        Charge
      Dining Room Reservations
  Shops
    Leases
      Rent
  Sleeping Accommodation
    Reservations
    Occupancy
      Charge

Meeting/Banquet Rooms
  Reservations
  Occupancy
    Charge
  Telephones
    Local
      Charge
    Long Distance
      Charge
  External Services
    Guided Tours
    Shopping
    Public Transit
    Airport Transportation
    Car Rental
Franchise Holder
  Franchise
    Franchise Fee
Customer
  Reservations
  Accounts Receivable Invoices
    Charge
Vendor
  Accounts Payable Invoices
    Accounts Payable Invoice Item
  Purchase Orders
    Purchase Order Item

APPENDIX A—TABLE 4 (TABLE 6.5)
Financial Entities

Department (Cost Center)
  Investments
  Assets
  Profit/Loss
  Transaction Type
    Budgeted Income
    Actual Income
      Charge
      Other Income
        Franchise Fees
        Rent
        Miscellaneous
    Budgeted Expenses
    Actual Expenses
      Salaries
      Taxes
      Benefits
      Pensions
      Purchases
        Purchase Order Item
        Accounts Payable Invoice Item
Chart of Accounts

APPENDIX A—TABLE 5
(TABLE 6.6)   Subject Data Bases

1 Location
2 Hotel Construction
3 Franchise Data
4 Staff Data
5 Equipment Data
6 Recreation
7 Shop
8 Sleeping Accommodation
9 Meeting/Banquet Room
10 Restaurant
11 External Services
12 Customer
13 Vendor
14 Financial
15 Tax Table
16 Maintenance (Work Schedule)
17 Telephone Service

APPENDIX A—TABLE 6 (TABLE 7.2)   Vacation
Hotels—Subject Data Bases

1 *Location*
Location
  Head Office
  Hotel
  New Hotel Site
2 *Hotel Construction*
New Hotel Site
  Plan
  Blueprint
  Building Permit
  Construction
3 *Franchise Data*
Hotel
Franchise Holder (Franchisee)
  Franchise
    Franchise Fee
4 *Staff Data*
Staff
  Salary
  Benefits
  Pension
  Education
  Work Schedule
5 *Equipment*
Equipment
  Equipment Reservation
  Equipment Rental
    Charge
  Inventory
6 *Recreation*
Recreation
  Swimming Pool
  Games
    Tennis
      Game Reservation
    Golf
      Game Reservation
    Other
      Game Reservation
  Gymnasium
7 *Shop*
Shop
  Lease
  Rent
8 *Sleeping Accommodation*
Sleeping Accommodation
  Reservation
  Occupancy
    Charge

APPENDIX A—TABLE 6 (TABLE 7.2)
(Continued)

9 *Meeting/Banquet Rooms*
   Meeting Banquet Room
      Reservation
      Occupancy
      Charge

10 *Restaurant*
    Restaurant
       Bar
          Meal
             Charge
       Coffee Shop
          Meal
             Charge
       Dining Room
          Meal
             Charge
          Dining Room Reservation

11 *External Services*
    External Services
       Guided Tour
       Shopping
       Public Transit
       Airport Transportation
       Car Rental

12 *Customer*
    Customer
       Reservation
       Accounts Receivable Invoice
          Charge

13 *Vendor*
    Vendor
       Accounts Payable Invoice
          Accounts Payable Item
       Purchase Order
          Purchase Order Item

14 *Financial Entities*
    Department (Cost Center)
       Investment
       Asset
       Profit/Loss
       Transaction Type
          Budgeted Income
          Actual Income
             Charge
          Other Income
             Franchise Fee
             Rent
             Miscellaneous

APPENDIX A—TABLE 6 (TABLE 7.2)
(Continued)

Budgeted Expenses
Actual Expenses
  Salary
  Taxes
  Benefits
  Pension
  Purchase
    Purchase Order Item
    Accounts Payable Invoice Item
 Chart of Accounts

15 *Tax Table*

16 *Maintenance*
Maintenance
 Laundry
 Work Schedule
  Room Cleaning
  Other

17 *Telephone*
Telephone
 Local
  Charge
 Long Distance
  Charge

APPENDIX A—TABLE 7 (TABLE 6.7)   Identifying
Business Applications

Sources: 1 Objectives and Critical Success Factors (CSFs)
        2 Functions
        3 Corporate Entity-Relationship Diagram

1 *Objectives and CSFs*

Marketing
Hotel Construction
Quality Control
Productivity Measurement

2 *Functions*

Financial
 Budget
 Payroll
 Accounts Receivable
 Accounts Payable
 General Ledger
 Investments
 Cash Management
 Purchasing
 Staff Pensions

APPENDIX A—TABLE 7 (TABLE 6.7) (*Continued*)

Marketing
  Sales
  Advertising
Hotel Construction
Franchise Sales
Franchise Management
  Quality Control
  Account Administration
  Building and Site Maintenance
Administration
  Staff
  Maintenance
Inventory Control
Equipment Rental
Reservations and Occupancy
Transportation
Shop Management
Restaurant Management
3 *Corporate Entity-Relationship Diagram*

Financial
  Budget
  Accounts Payable
  Accounts Receivable
  Purchasing
  Investments
  Payroll
  Pensions
  Tax Table
Franchise Management
Personnel
Hotel Construction
Sleeping Accommodation Reservations and Occupancy
Meeting/Banquet Room Reservations and Occupancy
Recreation
Shop Management
Restaurant Management
External Services
Customer Information
Vendor Information
Maintenance

APPENDIX A—TABLE 8 (TABLE 6.8) Consolidated and Refined
Business Applications (Head Office and Hotel)

Application	Head Off.	Hotel
01 Financial		
01 Budget	*	*
02 Payroll	*	*
03 Accounts Receivable	*	*
04 Accounts Payable	*	*
05 General Ledger	*	*
06 Investments	*	*
07 Cash Management	*	*
08 Purchasing	*	*
09 Staff Pensions	*	*
10 Tax Table	*	*
02 Marketing		
01 Sales	*	
02 Advertising	*	
03 Hotel Construction		
01 Hotel Construction	*	
04 Franchise Management		
01 Quality Control	*	
02 Account Administration	*	
03 Building and Site Maintenance	*	
04 Productivity Measurement	*	
05 Franchise Sales		
01 Franchise Sales	*	
06 Room Reservations and Occupancy		
01 Sleeping Accommodation	*	*
02 Meeting/Banquet Rooms	*	*
07 Equipment Management		
01 Inventory Control	*	*
02 Rental		*
08 Recreation		
01 Facility Reservations		*
09 Shop Management		
01 Shop Rental	*	*
10 Restaurant Management		
01 Reservations		*
11 External Services		
01 Transportation (Bus and Limousine)		*
02 Car Rental		*

APPENDIX A—TABLE 8 (TABLE 6.8) *(Continued)*

Application		Head Off.	Hotel
12	Customer		
	01 Customer	*	*
13	Vendor		
	01 Vendor	*	*
14	Administration		
	01 Staff	*	*
	02 Maintenance (Work Schedules)		*
	03 Telephone Services	*	*

APPENDIX A—TABLE 9 (TABLE 6.9) Consolidated and Refined Business Applications (Management, Information and Office Systems)

Application		Management Systems	Information Systems	Office Systems
01	Financial			
	01 Budget	*		*
	02 Payroll		*	
	03 Accounts Receivable		*	
	04 Accounts Payable		*	
	05 General Ledger		*	
	06 Investments		*	*
	07 Cash Management		*	
	08 Purchasing		*	
	09 Staff Pensions		*	
	10 Tax Table		*	
02	Marketing			
	01 Sales		*	
	02 Advertising		*	
03	Hotel Construction			
	01 Hotel Construction		*	
04	Franchise Management			
	01 Quality Control	*		
	02 Account Administration		*	
	03 Building and Site Maintenance		*	
	04 Productivity Measurement	*		
05	Franchise Sales			
	01 Franchise Sales		*	
06	Room Reservations and Occupancy			
	01 Sleeping Accommodation		*	
	02 Meeting/Banquet Rooms		*	
07	Equipment Management			
	01 Inventory Control		*	
	02 Rental		*	

APPENDIX A--TABLE 9 (TABLE 6.9) *(Continued)*

Application	Management Systems	Information Systems	Office Systems
08 Recreation			
01 Facility Reservations		*	
09 Shop Management			
01 Shop Rental		*	
10 Restaurant Management			
01 Reservations		*	
11 External Services			
01 Transportation (Bus and Limousine)		*	
02 Car Rental		*	
12 Customer			
01 Customer		*	
13 Vendor			
01 Vendor		*	
14 Administration			
01 Staff		*	
02 Maintenance (Work Schedules)		*	
03 Telephone Services		*	
15 Electronic Mail			*
16 Electronic Calendar			*
17 Decision Support	*		*

APPENDIX A—TABLE 10 (TABLE 6.10) Consolidated and Refined Business Applications Linked with Subject Data Bases

Application	Subject Create	Data Base Use
01 Financial		
01 Budget	14	14
02 Payroll	14	15,4
03 Accounts Receivable	14	12
04 Accounts Payable	14	13
05 General Ledger	14	14
06 Investments	14	14
07 Cash Management	14	14
08 Purchasing	14	14,13
09 Staff Pensions	14	14,4
10 Tax Table	15	
02 Marketing		
01 Sales		1,2,5,6,7,8, 9,10,11,12
02 Advertising		–do–

APPENDIX A—TABLE 10 (TABLE 6.10) (*Continued*)

Application	Subject Create	Data Base Use
03 Hotel Construction		
01 Hotel Construction	2	
04 Franchise Management		
01 Quality Control	3	8,9,10,11
02 Account Administration	3	
03 Building and Site Maintenance	3	
04 Productivity Measurement	3	8,9,10,11
05 Franchise Sales		
01 Franchise Sales	3	1,3
06 Room Reservations and Occupancy		
01 Sleeping Accommodation	8	12
02 Meeting/Banquet Rooms	9	12
07 Equipment Management		
01 Inventory Control	5	12
02 Rental	5	12
08 Recreation		
01 Facility Reservations	6	12
09 Shop Management		
01 Shop Rental	7	
10 Restaurant Management		
01 Reservations	10	12
11 External Services		
01 Transportation (Bus and Limousine)	11	12
02 Car Rental	11	12
12 Customer		
01 Customer	12	
13 Vendor		
01 Vendor	13	
14 Administration		
01 Staff	4	14
02 Maintenance (Work Schedules)	16	4
03 Telephone Services	17	12

APPENDIX A—TABLE 11 (TABLE 6.11) Subject Data Bases with
Related Applications

Subject Data Base	Application Create	Use
1 Location	03.01	02.01,02.02 05.01
2 Hotel Construction	03.01	02.01,02.02
3 Franchise Data	04.01–04.04, 05.01	05.01
4 Staff Data	14.01	01.02,01.09 14.02
5 Equipment Data	07.01,07.02	02.01,02.02
6 Recreation	08.01	02.01,02.02
7 Shop	09.01	02.01,02.02
8 Sleeping Accommodation	06.01	02.01,02.02 04.01–04.04
9 Meeting/Banquet Room	06.02	02.01,02.02 04.01–04.04
10 Restaurant	10.01	02.01,02.02 04.01,04.04
11 External Services	11.01,11.02	02.01,02.02 04.01–04.04
12 Customer	12.01	06.01,06.02 07.01,07.02 08.01,10.01 11.01,11.02 14.03
13 Vendor	13.01	01.04,01.08
14 Financial	01.01–01.09	01.01,01.05, 01.06,01.08 01.09,14.01
15 Tax Table	01.10	01.02
16 Maintenance (Work Schedule)	14.02	
17 Telephone Service	14.03	

APPENDIX A—TABLE 12 (TABLES 7.3–7.8 & TABLE 8.2)   Selected Subject Data Bases
Expanded and Shown in Canonical Form

	01 HOTEL (*Hotel Id*. Name, Address, Location, Telephone No., Telex No., No. of Bedrooms, No. of Meeting/Banquet Rooms, Hotel Open/Closed)
	03 SLEEPING ACCOMMODATION (*Hotel, Room No., Bedroom/Suite* Room Type, No. of Persons, Refrigerator, View)
	04 SLEEPING ACCOMMODATION RATE (*Hotel, Room No., Bedroom/Suite, Period* Single, Double, Additional Person)
Sleeping Accommodation/ Customer Relationship	05 S.A. RESERVATION (*Hotel, Room No., Bedroom/Suite, Customer Id., Reserv. Ref*. Arrival Date, No. of Persons, Arrival Time, Departure Date, Payment Method)
Sleeping Accommodation/ Customer Relationship	06 S.A. OCCUPANCY (*Hotel, Room No., Bedroom/Suite, Customer Id., Occup. Ref*. Occup. Date, Rate Discount, No. of Persons)
	07 MEETING/BANQUET ROOM (*Hotel, Room No., M/B Room* Room Type, No. of Persons, Features, View)
	08 MEETING/BANQUET ROOM RATE (*Hotel, Room No., M/B Room, Meal Income* M/B Room Rate)
Meeting/Banquet Room/Customer Relationship	09 M/B RESERVATION (*Hotel, Room No., M/B Room, Customer Id., Reserv. Ref*. Arrival Date, Time of Day, Departure Date, Payment Method, No. Attending, Table Type, Coffee Break, Lunch, Dinner)
Meeting/Banquet Room/Customer Relationship	10 M/B OCCUPANCY *Hotel, Room No., M/B Room, Customer Id., Occup. Ref*. Occup. Date, No. of Persons)
	11 EQUIPMENT (*Hotel, Equipment Type* Rate, No. in Stock)
Equipment/Customer Relationship	12 EQUIP RESERVATION (*Hotel, Customer Id., Equipment Type, Reserv. Ref*. Room No., Reserv. Date, Time of Day, Number Reserved)
Equipment/Customer Relationship	13 EQUIP RENTAL (*Hotel, Customer Id., Equipment Type, Rental Ref*. Room No., Rental Date, Number Rented)
Telephone/Room Rel.	14 TELEPHONE CALL (*Hotel, Room No., No. Called, Tel. Ref*. Call Date, Time, Local/Long Distance, No. of Minutes)
	15 DEPARTMENT (*Hotel, Cost Center* Name, Function)
	16 TRANSACTION TYPE (*Hotel, Cost Center, Trans. Type* Description)
Transaction Type/ COA Item/Business Transaction Relationship	17 GL LINE ITEM (*Hotel, Cost Center, Trans. Type, COA Item, Business Trans. Ref., GL Ref.*, Transaction Date, Advance/Charge, Invoice No.)

APPENDIX A—TABLE 12 (TABLES 7.3–7.8 & TABLE 8.2) *(Continued)*

18 CHART OF ACCOUNTS ITEM (*COA Item No.* Item Description)

Note: 1. The transaction type indicates whether the transaction is budgeted or actual, and expense or income.

2. The chart of accounts item identifies the account. Examples include:
- Sleeping Accommodation Reservation Advance
- Sleeping Accommodation Occupancy Charge
- Meeting/Banquet Room Reservation Advance
- Meeting/Banquet Room Occupancy Charge
- Equipment Charge
- Coffee Break Charge
- Meal Charge
- Telephone Call Charge
- Salary
- Overtime
- Benefits

The chart of accounts will probably be a hierarchy. Hence, the item no. will reflect the hierarchy levels. For example:

08 Sleeping Accommodation
    01 Sleeping Accommodation Advance
    02 Sleeping Accommodation Charge

3. The business transaction reference number has the same value as a reservation, occupancy, rental, and so on. Reference number provides the link between GL line item record and the business transaction records.

19 CUSTOMER (*Customer Id.,* Name, Address, Company, Business Address, Home Phone, Business Phone)

20 CREDIT CARD (*Customer Id., Company Credit Card No.* Expiry Date)

21 CUSTOMER INVOICE (*Invoice No.* Invoice Date, Customer Id.)

APPENDIX A—TABLE 13 (TABLE 8.3) Selections from Subject Data Bases—Event Table

Dynamic	Record Name	Data Element	Event Number	Event Description	Action/ Condition Number	Comment
A	Hotel	Name Address Location	01	Establish Hotel Rec.	01	—
D	Hotel	Name Address Location	02	Delete Hotel Record	02	—
M	Hotel	Telephone Number	03	Change Telephone Number	03	—
M	Hotel	Telex No.	04	Change Telex Number	04	—
M	Hotel	No. of Bedrooms	05	Change No. of Bedrooms	05	—
M	Hotel	No. of M/B Rooms	05a	Change No. of M/B Rooms	05	—
M	Hotel	Hotel open/ closed	06	Change Hotel Status	06 01	—
A	Room	Area	08a	Establish Room Rec.	01	—
D	Room	—	08b	Delete Room Rec.	06	—
A	Sleep. Accommo.	Room Type No. of Persons View	09	Estab. Sleep. Accommo. Rec.	01 05	—
D	Sleep. Accommo.	—	10	Delete Sleep. Accommo. Rec.	06	—
M	Sleep. Accommo.	Refrig.	11	Change Refrig. Status	09 10	—

APPENDIX A—TABLE 13 (TABLE 8.3) *(Continued)*

Dynamic	Record Name	Data Element	Event Number	Event Description	Action/ Condition Number	Comment
A	Sleep. Accommo. Rate	—	12	Estab. Sleep. Accommo. Rate Rec.	01	—
D	Sleep Accommo. Rate	—	13	Delete Sleep. Accommo. Rate Rec.	06	—
M	Sleep. Accommo. Rate	Single	14	Change Single Rate	11	—
M	Sleep. Accommo. Rate	Double	15	Change Double Rate	11	—
M	Sleep. Accommo. Rate	Additional Person	16	Change Add. Person Rate	11	—
A	Sl. Acc. Reservat.	—	17	Estab. S.A. Reservat. Record	12	—
D	Sl. Acc. Reservat.	—	18	Delete S.A. Reservat. Record	13 16	—
M	Sl. Acc. Reservat.	Arrival Date	18a	Change Arrival Date		—
M	Sl. Acc. Reservat.	No. of Persons	19	Change No. of Persons	14	—
M	Sl. Acc. Reservat.	Arrival Time	20	Change Arrival Time	14	—

	Entity	Action			Field	
M	Sl. Acc. Reservat.	Change Depart. Date	14	21	Departure Date	—
M	Sl. Acc. Reservat.	Change Payment Method	14	22	Payment Method	—
A	Sl. Acc. Occup.	Estab. Sl. Acc. Occup. Rec.	15	24	—	—
D	Sl. Acc. Occup.	Delete Sl. Acc. Occup. Rec.	16	25	—	—
M	Sl. Acc. Occup.	Change Date	16a	25a	Date	—
M	Sl. Acc. Occup.	Change Rate Discount	17	26	Rate Discount	—
M	Sl. Acc. Occup.	Change No. of Persons	18	27	No. of Persons	—
A	Meet./Banquet Room	Estab. Meet./Banquet Room Record	01 05	29	Room Type No. of Persons View	—
D	Meet./Banquet Room	Delete Meet./Banquet Room Record	06	30	—	—
M	Meet./Banquet Room	Change Meet./Banquet Room Features	19	31	Features	—
A	Meet./Banquet Rm. Rate	Estab. M/B Room Rate Record	01	32	—	—
D	Meet./Banquet Rm. Rate	Delete M/B Room Rate Record	06	33	—	—
M	Meet./Banquet Rm. Rate	Change M/B Room Rate	20	34	M/B Room Rate	—
A	Meet./Banquet Rm. Reser.	Estab. M/B Room Reser. Record	21	35	—	—

APPENDIX A—TABLE 13 (TABLE 8.3) *(Continued)*

Dynamic	Record Name	Data Element	Event Number	Event Description	Action/Condition Number	Comment
D	Meet./Banquet Rm. Reser.	—	36	Delete M/B Room Reser. Record	22 26	—
M	Meet./Banquet Rm. Reser.	Arrival Date	36a	Change Arrival Date	23	—
M	Meet./ Banquet Rm. Reser.	Time of Day	37	Change Time of Day	23	—
M	Meet./Banquet Rm. Reser.	Depart. Date	38	Change Depart. Date	23	—
M	Meet./Banquet Rm. Reser.	Payment Method	39	Change Payment Method	23	—
M	Meet./Banquet Rm. Reser.	Number Attend.	40	Change Number Attending	23	—
M	Meet./Banquet Rm. Reser.	Table Type	41	Change Table Type	23	—
M	Meet./Banquet Rm. Reser.	Coffee Break	42	Change Coffee Break	23	—
M	Meet./Banquet Rm. Reser.	Lunch	43	Change Lunch	23	—
M	Meet./Banquet Rm. Reser.	Dinner	44	Change Dinner	23	—
A	Meet./Banquet Rm. Occup.	—	47c	Estab. M/B Room Occup. Record	25	—
D	Meet./Banquet Rm. Occup.	—	48	Delete M/B Room Occup. Record	26	—
M	Meet./Banquet Rm. Occup.	Date	71	Change Date	37	—

M	Meet./Banquet Rm. Occup.	No. of Persons	48a	Change No. of Persons	25a
A	Equipment	—	85	Estab. Equip. Rec.	45
D	Equipment	—	86	Delete Equip. Rec.	46
M	Equipment	Equip. Rate	87	Change Equip. Rate	24
M	Equipment	No. in Stock	88	Change No. in Stock	48
A	Equip. Reservation	—	46	Estab. Equip. Reser.	21
D	Equip. Reservation	—	47	Delete Equip. Reser.	22
M	Equip. Reservation	Room No.	47b	Change Room No.	23
M	Equip. Reservat.	Date	47c	Change Date	23
M	Equip. Reservat.	Time of Day	47d	Change Time of Day	23
M	Equip. Reservat.	Number Reser.	47a	Change Number Reser.	23
A	Equip. Rental	Room No. / Date / No. Rented	47e	Estab. Equip. Rental Rec.	49
D	Equip. Rental	—	47f	Delete Equip. Rental Rec.	50
A	Telephone Call	Date / Time / Local/Long Dist. / No. of Minutes	56	Estab. Teleph. Rec.	30
D	Telephone Call	—	57	Delete Teleph. Rec.	31

Dynamic	Record Name	Data Element	Event Number	Event Description	Action/ Condition Number	Comment
A	Dept.	Name Function	07	Establish Dept. Record	07	—
D	Dept.	—	08	Delete Dept. Record	08	—
A	Trans. Type	Descript.	72	Est. Trans. Type Rec.	07	—
D	Trans. Type	—	73	Delete Trans. Type Rec.	08	—
A	Chart of Accts. Item	Item Desc	74	Est. Chart of Accounts Item Record	01	—
D	Chart of Accts. Item	—	75	Delete Chart of Accounts Item Rec.	06	—
A	Inv. Line Item	—	76	Add Inv. Line Item Rec.	38	—
D	Inv. Line Item	—	77	Delete Inv. Line Item Rec.	39	—
M	Inv. Line Item	Date	78	Change Date	40	—
M	Inv. Line Item	Advance/Charge	79	Modify Invoice/Charge	41	—
M	Inv. Line Item	Invoice No.	80	Add Invoice No.	35	—
A	Customer	Name	59	Estab. Cust. Record	12 15 21 25	If no reservat. If no reservat.

	Entity	Ref.	Operation	Attribute	Keys	Notes
D	Customer	60	Delete Cust. Record	—	13 22 34	—
M	Customer	61	Change Cust. Address	Address	33	—
M	Customer	62	Change Co.	Company	33	—
M	Customer	63	Change Bus. Address	Business Address	33	—
M	Customer	64	Change Home Phone	Home Phone	33	—
M	Customer	65	Change Bus. Phone	Business Phone	33	—
A	Customer Credit Card	66	Estab. Cust. Credit Card Record	—	12 15 21 25	— If no reservat. If no reservat.
D	Customer Credit Card	67	Delete Cust. Credit Card Record	—	13 22	—
M	Customer Credit Card	68	Change Expiry Date	Expiry Date	33	If change during stay in hotel
A	Customer Invoice	69	Estab. Cust. Invoice Rec.	Date Cust. Id.	35	—
D	Customer Invoice	70	Delete Cust. Invoice Rec.	—	36	—

Note: This analysis is based on the hotel subject data bases which have been expanded and normalized. Relationship entities include all keys from the parent entities in the relationship entity key. In most real-life situations, the relationship entity is identified by a unique reference number. When this occurs, the parent entity keys become foreign keys in each record. These parent entity foreign keys *must* be included when the record is established.

Update Application	Action/ Condition Number	Action/ Condition Description	Dynamic	Event Number	Event Description	Organization Responsible
4.2 Fran. Mgmt.— Acct. Admin.	01	When new hotel opened	A	01	Establish Hotel Rec.	Head Office
			A	08a	Establish Room Rec.	
			A	09	Estab. Sl. Accommo. Rec.	
			A	12	Estab. Sl. Accommo. Rate Record	
			A	29	Estab. Meet./Banquet Room Record	
			A	32	Estab. Meet./Banquet Room Rate Rec.	
			A	74	Est. Chart of Accounts Item Record	
	02	When inf. on closed hotel is no longer reqd.	D	02	Delete Hotel Record	
	03	If hotel telephone no. changed	M	03	Change Teleph. No.	
	04	If hotel telex no. changed	M	04	Change Telex Number	
	05	If hotel expanded	M	05	Change No. of Bedrooms	

Section	Condition		Code	No.	Description
			M	05a	Change No. of M/B Rooms
			A	09	Estab. Sleep. Accommo. Rec.
			A	29	Estab. Meet./Banquet Room Record
06	If hotel closed		M	06	Change Hotel Status
			D	08b	Delete Room Record
			D	10	Delete Sleep. Accommo. Rec.
			D	13	Delete Sleep. Accommo. Rate Record
			D	30	Delete Meet./Banquet Room Record
			D	33	Delete M/B Rate Rec.
			D	75	Delete Chart of Accounts Item Rec.
1.3 Fin.— Acct.s Receivable 07	When a new Dept. is established	Head Off.	A	07	Establish Dept. Record
			A	72	Est. Trans. Type Rec.
08	When inf. on dept. no longer reqd.		D	08	Delete Dept. Record
			D	73	Delete Trans. Type Rec.

Update Application	Action/ Condition Number	Action/ Condition Description	Dynamic	Event Number	Event Description	Organization Responsible
6.1 Room Reser. Occup.— Sleep. Accom.	09	When refrig. added to sl. accommo.	M	11	Change Refrig. Status	Sleeping Accommo. Admin.
	10	When refrig. removed from sl. accommo.	M	11	Change Refrig. Status	
	11	When sleep. accommo. rates change	M	14	Change Single Rate	
			M	15	Change Double Rate	
			M	16	Change Add. Person Rate	
	12	When sleep. accommo. reservation received	A	17	Estab. Sl. Accommo. Reservation Record	Sl. Accommo. Admin. and Head Office Admin.
			A	59	Estab. Cust. Record	
			A	66	Estab. Cust. Credit Card Record	
			Report		Reser. Confirm. to Customer	
	13	When sleep. accommo. cancellation received	D	18	Delete Sl. Accommo. Reser. Rec.	
			D	60	Delete Cust. Credit Card Record	

Process	No.	Condition	Type	ID	Data Change	Destination
	14	When sleep. accommo. reservation changed	M	18a	Change Arrival Date	
			M	19	Change No. of Persons	
6.1 Room Reserv. Occup.—Sleeping Accommo. and			M	20	Change Arrival Time	
12.1 Cust.			M	21	Change Depart. Date	
			M	22	Change Payment Method	
			Report		Reserv. Change to Cust.	Sleeping Accommo. Admin.
	15	When sleep. accommo. occupied	A	24	Estab. Sl. Accommo. Occup. Record	
			A	59	Estab. Cust. Record	
			A	66	Est. Cust. Credit Card Record	
4.2 Fran. Mgmt.—Acct. Admin.	16	When sl. accommo. info. no longer reqd. by law	D	25	Delete Sl. Accommo. Occup. Rec.	Head Off.
			D	18	Delete Sl. Accommo. Reser. Rec.	
6.1 Room Reser. Occup.—Sl. Accom.	16a	If S.A. Occup. date changed	M	25a	Change Date	Sl. Acc. Admin.
	17	If sleep. accommo. rate discount changed	M	26	Change Rate Discount	
	18	If no. of persons occup. sleep. accommo. Changes	M	27	Change No. of Persons	

Update Application	Action/ Condition Number	Action/ Condition Description	Dynamic	Event Number	Event Description	Organization Responsible
6.2 Room Reser. Occup. Meet./Banq. Rm.	19	If meet./banquet room features change	M	31	Change Meet./Banquet Room Features	Meet./Banquet Room Admin.
	20	If meet./banquet room rate changes	M	34	Change Meet./Banquet Room Rate	
	21	When meet./banquet room reservation received	A	35	Estab. Meet./Banquet Room Reser. Rec.	Meet./Banq. Room Admin. and Head Off. Admin.
			A	46	Estab. Meet./Banq. Room Equip. Reser. Record	
			A	59	Estab. Cust. Record	
			A	66	Estab. Cust. Credit Card Record	
			Report		Reser. Confirm. to Cust.	
	22	When meet./banquet room cancellation received	D	36	Delete Meet./Banq. Room Record.	

Type	No.	Operation	Condition
D	47	Delete Meet./Banq. Room Equip. Reser. Record	
D	60	Delete Cust. Record	
D	67	Delete Cust. Credit Card Record	
M	36a	Change Arrival Date	
M	37	Change Time of Day	
M	38	Change Depart. Date	
M	39	Change Payment Method	
M	40	Change Number Attending	
M	41	Change Table Type	
M	42	Change Coffee Break	
M	43	Change Lunch	
M	44	Change Dinner	
M	47a	Change No. of Equip. Reser.	23 — When meet./banq. room reservation changed
M	47b	Change Room No.	
M	47c	Change Date	
M	47d	Change Time of Day	
Report		Change Confirm. to Cust.	

APPENDIX A—TABLE 14 (TABLE 8.4) (*Continued*)

Update Application	Action/Condition Number	Action/Condition Description	Dynamic	Event Number	Event Description	Organization Responsible
7.2 Equip. Mgmt.—Rental	45	When equip. acquired	A	85	Estab. Equip. Record	Meet./Banq. Room Admin.
	46	When equip. no longer stocked	D	86	Delete Equip. Record	
	24	When equip. rate changed	M	47b	Change Equip. Rate	
	48	When stock changed	M	88	Change Number in Stock	
	49	When equip. rented	A	47e	Estab. Equip. Rental Rec.	
	50	When equip. rental inf. no longer reqd.	D	47f	Delete Equip. Rental Rec.	
6.2 Room Reser. Occup.— Meet./ Banq. Room and	25	When meet./banquet room occup.	A	47c	Estab. Meet./Banq. Room Occup. Rec.	Meet./Banq. Room Admin.
12.1 Cust.			A	59	Estab. Cust. Record	
			A	66	Estab. Cust. Credit Card Record	
	37	When M/B occup. date changed	M	71	Change Date	
	25a	When meet./banq. room occup. changes	M	48a	Change No. of Persons	
4.2 Fran. Mgmt.—Acct. Admin.	26	When meet./banq. room occup. info. no longer reqd. by law	D	48	Delete Meet./Banq. Room Occup. Rec.	Head Off.
			D	36	Delete	

Ref	Process	No.	Condition	No.	Type	Record	Responsible
						Meet./Banq. Room Reser. Rec.	
14.3	Admin.—Teleph. Services	30	When telephone call made	56	A	Estab. Telephone Record	Telephone Admin.
		31	When telephone record no longer reqd. by law	57	D	Delete Telephone Record	
1.3	Finance—Accounts Receivable	38	When charge made	76	A	Establish Charge Rec.	All Depts.
		39	When account. info. no longer reqd. by law	77	D	Delete Charge Record.	Head Off.
		40	If charge date not correct	78	M	Change Date	All Depts.
		41	If charge not correct	79	M	Modify Charge	
		35	When cust. is charged for services	69	A	Estab. Cust. Invoice Rec.	Hotel Admin.
				80	M Report	Add Invoice No. Invoice to Customer	
12.1	Cust.	33	If customer info. changes	61	M	Change Cust. Address	Sleeping Accommo. or Meet./Banq. Room Admin.
				62	M	Change Co.	
				63	M	Change Bus. Address	
				64	M	Change Phone Number	
				65	M	Change Business Phone Number	
				68	M	Change Credit Card Expiry Date	
12.1	Cust.	34	When cust. rec. no longer reqd. by law	60	D	Delete Cust. Record	Head Off.
		36	When cust. invoice rec. no longer required by law	70	D	Delete Cust. Invoice Record	Head Off.

APPENDIX A—TABLE 15 (TABLE 3.2)
Menu Hierarchy Based on Function

Menu Level 1—Function

01 Finance
02 Marketing
03 Hotel Construction
04 Franchise Management
05 Franchise Sales
06 Room Reservations and Occupancy
07 Equipment Management
08 Recreation
09 Shop Management
10 Restaurant Management
11 External Services
12 Customer
13 Vendor
14 Administration

APPENDIX A—TABLE 16 (TABLE 9.3)   Menu
Hierarchy Based on Function

Menu Level 2—Application

Function—01 Finance

01 Budget
02 Payroll
03 Accounts Receivable
04 Accounts Payable
05 General Ledger
06 Investments
07 Cash Management
08 Purchasing
09 Staff Pensions
10 Tax Tables

Function 04—Franchise Management

01 Quality Control
02 Account Administration
03 Building and Site Maintenance
04 Productivity Measurement

Function 06—Room Reservation and Occupancy

01 Sleeping Accommodation
02 Meeting/Banquet Rooms

Function 07—Equipment Management

01 Inventory Control
02 Rental

APPENDIX A—TABLE 16 (TABLE 9.3)
(Continued)

Function 12—Customer
01 Customer

Function 14—Administration
01 Staff
02 Maintenance (day-to-day operations)
03 Telephone Services

APPENDIX A—TABLE 17 (TABLE 9.4) Menu Hierarchy Based
on Function

Menu Level 3—Procedure Group
Application 04.02 Franchise Management—Account Administration
01 External Actions/Conditions
02 Records Created (Updated)
03 Records Used (Accessed) but Not Created (Updated)
04 Outputs

APPENDIX A—TABLE 18 (TABLE 9.5) Menu Hierarchy Based on Function

Menu Level 4—Procedure
Application 04.02 Franchise Management—Account Administration
Procedure Group 04.02.01—External Actions and Conditions
01 When new hotel opened
02 When information on closed hotel is no longer required
03 If hotel telephone number is changed
04 If hotel telex number is changed
05 If hotel is expanded
06 If hotel is closed
16 When sleeping accommodation is no longer required by law
26 When meeting/banquet room occupancy information is no longer required by law
91 Annually

APPENDIX A—TABLE 19 (TABLE 9.6)   Menu Hierarchy Based on Function

Menu Level 5—Function Event Module

Application 04.02 Franchise Management—Account Administration

Function Event Module 04.02.01.01—When new hotel opened

01	Establish hotel record
08a	Establish room record
09	Establish sleeping accommodation record
12	Establish sleeping accommodation rate
29	Establish meeting/banquet room record
32	Establish meeting/banquet room rate

Function Event Module 04.02.01.02—When information on closed hotel is no longer required

02	Delete hotel record

Function Event Module 04.02.01.03—If hotel telephone number is changed

03	Change telephone number

Function Event Module 04.02.01.04—If hotel telex number is changed

04	Change telex number

Function Event Module 04.02.01.05—If hotel is expanded

05	Change number of bedrooms
05a	Change number of meeting/banquet rooms
09	Establish sleeping accommodation record
29	Establish meeting/banquet room record

Function Event Module 04.02.01.06—If hotel is closed

06	Change hotel status
08b	Delete room record
10	Delete sleeping accommodation record
13	Delete sleeping accommodation rate record
30	Delete meeting/banquet room record
33	Delete meeting/banquet room rate record

Function Event Module 04.02.01.16—When sleeping accommodation information is no longer required by law

18	Delete sleeping accommodation reservation record
25	Delete sleeping accommodation occupancy record

Function Event Module 04.02.01.26—When meeting/banquet room information is no longer required by law

36	Delete meeting/banquet room reservation record
48	Delete meeting/banquet room occupancy record

Function Event Module 04.02.01.91—Annually

Report 01	Potential annual sleeping accommodation and meeting/banquet room income by hotel
Report 02	Maximum daily occupancy by hotel
Report 03	Franchise holder and annual franchise fees by hotel

APPENDIX A—TABLE 20 (TABLE 9.7)   Menu Hierarchy Based on Function

Menu Level 6—Input Screens and Reports
Application 04.02 Franchise Management—Account Administration

---

04.02.01.01.01   HOTEL

Hotel Identification Number _____

Hotel Name _____

Address _____

_____

_____

_____

Location _____

Telephone Number _____

Telex Number _____

Number of Rooms _____

Hotel Open/Closed _____

04.02.01.91
Potential Annual Sleeping Accommodation and Meeting/Banquet Room Income by
Hotel

Hotel	No. of Bedrooms	No. of M/B Rooms	Total Annual Income
_____	_____	_____	_____
_____	_____	_____	_____
_____	_____	_____	_____
_____	_____	_____	_____

APPENDIX B
The STRIPE Methodology—
Table of Contents
Planning Levels, Phases
and Activities

The Strategic Information Resource Plan (SIRP) Process

Phase SUP   Start-up Phase

Activities

SUP.1   Conduct STRIPE Management Seminar
SUP.2   Establish the SIRP Administrative Framework
SUP.3   Conduct a Review Session
SUP.3   Conduct STRIPE Workshop

Phase SP1   The Business Strategy

Activities

SP1.A   Develop Business Strategy Phase Plan
SP1.B   Conduct a Planning Session
SP1.1   Define the Business Strategy
SP1.X   Prepare Business Strategy Phase Report
SP1.Y   Conduct Review Session
SP1.Z   Modify Business Strategy Phase Report

Phase SP2   The Information Architecture

Activities

SP2.A   Develop Information Architecture Phase Plan
SP2.B   Conduct a Planning Session
SP2.1   Identify the Organization's Functions

The Tactical Planning Process

The Operational Planning Process

Phase OP1   Individual Project Plans
Activities
OP1.1   Develop Individual Project Plans

Phase OP2   Business System Specification
Activities
OP2.1   Define Activity Level Functions
OP2.2   Define Output Requirements
OP2.3   Design the Output Formats

Phase OP3   Procedure Design
Activities
OP3.1   Analyze Events and External Actions/Conditions
OP3.2   Define Procedures
OP3.3   Design Menu Hierarchies
OP3.4   Design Input Screens and Formats

Phase OP4   Physical Data Base Design
Activities
OP4.1   Expand Data to the Activity Level Functions
OP4.2   Confirm that Data to Provide the Outputs Identified in OP2.2 are Defined
OP4.3   Analyze Data Usage in Terms of Volumes and Accesses
OP4.4   Design Physical Data Bases
OP4.5   Design and Develop Data Base Access Modules

Phase OP5   Procedure Expansion
Activities
OP5.1   Develop File Update Logic
OP5.2   Develop Output Logic

Phase OP6   System Construction
Activities
OP6.1   Design Physical Procedures
OP6.2   Code Physical Procedures
OP6.3   Test Physical Procedures

Phase OP7   System Test
Activities
OP7.1   Prepare MIS and User Test Cases and Test Data
OP7.2   MIS Test System
OP7.3   User Test System

Phase OP8   Application Package Acquisition
Activities
OP8.1   Define Functional and Data Requirements
OP8.2   Evaluate Off-the-shelf versus Turnkey Products
OP8.3   Cost Justify Package Acquisition

Index

Announcing. . . .

The Annual Prentice Hall Professional/Technical/Reference Catalog: Books For Computer Scientists, Computer/Electrical Engineers and Electronic Technicians

- Prentice Hall, the leading publisher of Professional/Technical/Reference books in the world, is pleased to make its vast selection of titles in computer science, computer/electrical engineering and electronic technology more accessible to all professionals in these fields through the publication of this new catalog!

- If your business or research depends on timely, state-of-the-art information, The Annual Prentice Hall Professional/Technical/Reference Catalog: Books For Computer Scientists, Computer/Electrical Engineers and Electronic Technicians was designed especially for you! Titles appearing in this catalog will be grouped according to interest areas. Each entry will include: title, author, author affiliations, title description, table of contents, title code, page count and copyright year.

- In addition, this catalog will also include advertisements of new products and services from other companies in key high tech areas.

SPECIAL OFFER!

- Order your copy of The Annual Prentice Hall Professional/Technical/Reference Catalog: Books For Computer Scientists, Computer/Electrical Engineers and Electronic Technicians for only $2.00 and receive $5.00 off the purchase of your first book from this catalog. In addition, this catalog entitles you to special discounts on Prentice Hall titles in computer science, computer/electrical engineering and electronic technology.

Please send me _____ copies of The Annual Prentice Hall Professional/Technical/Reference Catalog (title code: 62280-3)

SAVE!

If payment accompanies order, plus your state's sales tax where applicable, Prentice Hall pays postage and handling charges. Same return privilege refund guaranteed. Please do not mail cash.

- ☐ PAYMENT ENCLOSED—shipping and handling to be paid by publisher (please include your state's tax where applicable).
- ☐ BILL ME for The Annual Prentice Hall Professional/Technical/Reference Catalog (with small charge for shipping and handling).

Mail your order to: Prentice Hall, Book Distribution Center,
Route 59 at Brook Hill Drive,
West Nyack, N.Y. 10994

Name _____

Address _____

City _____ State _____ Zip _____

I prefer to charge my ☐ Visa   ☐ MasterCard

Card Number _____ Expiration Date _____

Signature _____

Offer not valid outside the United States.

Dept. 1

D-PPTR-CS(9)